MEDITATION: THE INWARD ART

Meditation: the Inward Art

BY BRADFORD SMITH

J. B. Lippincott Company
PHILADELPHIA
AND NEW YORK

Contents

"Let the words of my mouth, and the meditation of my heart, be acceptable in thy sight, O Lord, my strength, and my redeemer." Ps. 19:14.

MEDITATION: THE INWARD ART

1

WHAT IS MEDITATION?

TO every man comes a time when he must face himself, but often it comes too late. The devices we have for avoiding this confrontation are many, and we are clever at finding them all. No chore seems harder than to look inward. Yet everyone who wants to live up to the standard of human possibility needs to look within. To open the door to this inner world, all we need is silence and a stout will. These together make meditation—it is as simple as that. And as difficult. To learn the art of confronting ourselves before it is too late —and to do this every day—is to discover a source of strength as wonderful as it is accessible.

We often say that we envy those who have time to savor life and to reflect upon its meaning, yet anyone who steadfastly sets aside fifteen minutes a day for meditation can have this rich advantage, and strengthen his life with it so that every experience has a richer flavor and every action firm roots. There is no need to envy those who travel to far places, for the human mind employed in solitude is infinite in resourcefulness. In the orbit of the mind exploring the vastness of intellectual space lies an adventure as exciting as orbiting in a space capsule.

Why meditate?

Meditation is good in and for itself because it is an active working of the whole personality—emotions, intellect, spirit. More, it draws the isolated individual into the universal and makes the connection so clear that no one who learns the art of meditation can ever feel alone or isolated in a hostile universe.

But what is meditation?

It is Henry David Thoreau building his cabin on the edge of Walden Pond and so arranging his life that he had time for both the great and the little, the way of the universe and the way of ants and squirrels, and time to discover the unity of star and snake, of pond and Milky Way.

It is Ralph Waldo Emerson tramping through the woods near Concord, then sitting in his book-lined study to write in his Journal:

"It is very easy in the world to live by the opinion of the world. It is very easy in solitude to be self-centered. But the finished man is he who in the midst of the crowd keeps with perfect sweetness the independence of solitude."

Or this, written at sea in 1833:

"A man contains all that is needful to his government within himself. He is made a law unto himself. All real good or evil that can befall him must be from himself. . . . The purpose of life seems to be to acquaint man with himself. He is not to live to the future as described to him, but to live in the real future by living to the real present. The highest revelation is that God is in every man."

Meditation implies a concern with fundamental things, but does not limit or define them. One may come through meditation to a sense of the presence of God as a real and living person, a kind of super-father. Or the sense of presence may come as a merging with the world of nature until one feels caught up in its processes and becomes one with sunlight and wind and birdsong and clouds floating. Or a sense of well-being may flood into the consciousness and irradiate it with a conviction of the presence of goodness—the goodness of life, of experience, of friendship and childhood and love. Or the sense of unity with something beyond self may come as a sensation of light flooding inward—through closed eyelids into the quiet and receptive mind, into every cavern and nerve of the body. Or it may be simply a feeling of peace and contentment.

In any case, it relates the self, the individual to something beyond and outside, something which seemed alien but which in the moment of insight becomes organically related, interfused.

SOME DEFINITIONS

There is nothing mysterious about meditation—not in the way of entering into it at any rate. We shall soon begin with a few exercises. But first, it will be helpful to look at the word itself.

The root "med-" is the same as in "medical," and originally meant to measure (as in the word "mete"), to consider, to reflect. It seems to be related to a Greek root meaning to care for, attend to, study or practise.

Here are three dictionary definitions of meditation:

"Sustained reflection; the turning or revolving of a subject in the mind; close or continued thought."

"A private devotional act, consisting in deliberate reflection upon some spiritual truth or mystery, accompanied by mental prayer and . . . resolutions as to future conduct. . . . Its principal object is not to acquire knowledge, but to advance in love of God and holiness of life."

"A private religious or devotional exercise consisting in a continuous application of the mind to the consideration of some religious or moral truth, or the like, in order to promote personal holiness or love of God."

Most of our thinking is directed at problem-solving; in fact, this was John Dewey's definition of the act of thought. A tool breaks, and we patch it with tape or wire in such a way that it will work again. A baby cries, and we lift him up to change or feed him. The roof leaks, and we plug the hole. Meditation, obviously, differs from this.

13

Meditation: The Inward Art

Another kind of thinking, and perhaps the most prevalent, is daydreaming. In these waking fantasies we see ourselves achieving the success that eludes us in reality, taking a sweet revenge on someone who has offended us, winning praise for a courageous or selfless act, or just planting the garden we never get around to, or being loved and understood. Meditation is not this.

Still another way of thought is contemplation. The "temple" which forms the middle of the word really belongs there, for in Rome the *contemplum* was the space in the temple which the diviners marked off as the spot from which the observations of the auguries were made. Originally the *templum* was simply an open place set apart for the observation of the flight of birds, whose motions signified good or evil fortune. So contemplation, originally, was a matter of very attentive and sometimes prolonged observation.

By extension, the word came to mean the act of holding an idea continuously before the mind. Locke defines it as "keeping the idea which is brought into [the mind] for some time actually in view."

This does not seem very far from meditation. But Jeremy Taylor makes a further distinction. "Meditations in order to a good life, let them be as exalted as the capacity of the person and subject will endure up to the height of contemplation; but if contemplation comes to be a distinct thing and something besides or beyond a distinct degree of virtuous meditation, it is lost to all sense, and religion and prudence."

This may sound mysterious. What Jeremy Taylor fears is a transport of religious emotionalism which takes leave of the rational faculty. He uses the word "contemplation," probably with some medieval practitioner in mind, to express a state beyond meditation, beyond intellectual control. Perhaps the man he had in mind was Richard of Saint Victor, a twelfth-century mystic whom Dante praised and whose works had a renewed vogue in

Taylor's time.

Richard in his *Benjamin Minor* makes a very clear distinction between meditation and contemplation—one that our modern dictionaries have given up. A truly medieval mind, he binds all his ideas to the Bible and thus makes the abstract tangible through allegory. Benjamin is therefore his symbol for contemplation, Joseph for meditation.

"By Benjamin we understand the kind of contemplation which deals with invisible things, by Joseph, meditation about moral issues," he says. "For the understanding of invisible things belongs to the pure intelligence, but consideration of morals belongs to true prudence." (Chapter 87.)

In his principal work, *Benjamin Major,* Richard carries the distinction further. "Meditation with great mental industry, plods along the steep and laborious road keeping the end in view. Contemplation on a free wing, circles around with great nimbleness wherever the impulse takes it. . . . Meditation investigates, contemplation wonders. . . . Meditation arises from the reason, contemplation from the intelligence. . . . Meditation is perseveringly intent on one thing only. Contemplation sheds the light of a single ray upon innumerable objects." (Chap. 3.)

And again: "Contemplation has one purpose, meditation another. The work of meditation is to seek out hidden things, that of contemplation to wonder at clear truths."

There is no point in getting bogged down in technicalities, so it will be enough to say that by reason Richard refers to the power of comprehending and applying logical thought, while by intelligence he means the quality of understanding or knowing.

Meditation as we shall deal with it includes both the laborious road and the free wing, both the patient exploration by reason and logic and the quick surmise and sudden perception of intuition, leading to that inflooding of light and peace which in its strongest form is known as ecstasy.

Meditation is not figuring how to raise profits or planning a trip south or even working out a plan that will benefit the community. It is an effort which concentrates all the faculties on harmonizing the individual with the universe.

SOME PLAIN EXAMPLES

If you are daydreaming, you might muse: "I shall write a book and become famous." If contemplating: "My book will deal with speech, this marvelous faculty which joins man to God." Prayer: "Give me strength and wit and skill to accomplish the task I have set myself, and if it is Thy will, let me bring it to completion." But meditation might go something like this:

" 'In the beginning was the Word, and the Word was with God, and the Word was God.' (John 1:1.) How shall I understand this? How can the Word be God? Can it mean that before creation there had to be a concept, a plan, a mind? And that the Word is the means, the bridge by which concept becomes fact? Is it that the order we find in all nature points to—or is of itself—an order based in reason? Is God the reason, the order we find in the universe? What did John mean by the Word? No doubt he was influenced by the Greeks, the Stoics, Philo, and most of all perhaps by Genesis: 'And God said, Let there be light: and there was light.'

"The Word, then, could be the creative power, the divine energy—the source of life and love and light. And man, who of all the creation has language, through language knows the mind of the Maker. Out of His mind came creation. How do I know this? Only that the creation is incredibly planned and patterned, beyond anything my small mind can grasp. But because I too have mind, and because with words I can grasp at some edges of the greater mystery, I see mind—order, sequence, repetition according to pattern, law and ordered succession—in every corner of the creation, from star to snowflake, from the curving of space to the curves that make for beauty.

16

"Much of this is beyond understanding, but by naming things I can capture them, and my little words give back some small echo of the Word. The echo is enough for me; my ears are not tuned to the larger thunder, and I must learn to be content with the wavelengths they respond to. It is enough to teach me that the Word—the power to think, to reason, to wonder, to explore, and sometimes to know—binds me to the Maker and to all that is.

"What I would do, I must first utter, even if it be in the silent caverns of the mind. For in the beginning was the Word."

I have tried to set down here, without premeditation (except insofar as I have always wondered about these things) and without correction, a train of ideas as they sprang into the mind. This, whether better or worse, is an act of meditation, and here is the raw result. It might have come out a lot better or a lot worse. But this is the sort of thing, or one sort of thing, that meditation produces. Each individual, starting from the same place, would take a different path.

There is only one God who lives, and that is the one you find within. We have a curious habit of assuming that God is still what He was to us in the first grade at Sunday school. We think we outgrow him. Instead, we carry our first-grade concept along with us into maturity and fail to outgrow that. Then we blame God. The way to find Him is through meditation—this is the only way. His word, speaking through your mind. No matter what church you follow or do not follow, you believe in something. All too probably, you have not stopped long enough or probed deep enough to see what it is. So you have fallen short of realizing yourself as a person.

One of the finest things in all literature happens almost unnoticed in the middle of the Twenty-third Psalm. After that tranquil beginning, "The Lord is my shepherd; I shall not want," there follows a beautiful description of the Lord's leading and caring, all in the third person. "He leadeth me beside the still

waters; he restoreth my soul." But when danger threatens—
"Yea, though I walk through the valley of the shadow of death"
—and the sure response comes, "I will fear no evil," there follows that incredibly beautiful and natural turning from the third
to the second person: "For thou art with me."

There is no more perfect meditation than this Psalm; perhaps
it can teach us all we need to know about the art of meditating.
For this surely is the deep purpose and the sweet gift of meditation: "Thou art with me." To know that the individual is not
alone, but is tied to the whole creation and creator—to bring the
self into focus with the all—this is the goal of spiritual meditation. Hindu teachers speak of "this" and "that"—this, the individual soul; that, the universal soul. The whole practice of Hindu
meditation, of Yoga, is to reach the goal of knowing merely "This
is that," but knowing it certainly, firmly. When we learn that
His law is our freedom—"thy rod and thy staff they comfort
me"—then we are able to say: "My cup runneth over." It is
this running over of the cup that one feels when meditation has
been truly and faithfully practised.

"Surely goodness and mercy shall follow me all the days of
my life, and I will dwell in the house of the Lord for ever."

THE UNIVERSAL STREAM

Man is umbilical to earth, but is forever cutting the vital cord.
He is born free, but is chained by iron of his own forging and
locked in a cell to which he alone holds the key.

Man is related to the universe—plain common sense shows
him that. His relatives are not only his sisters and his cousins
and his aunts, but the stars in their courses, the darting, submicroscopic elements of the atom moving within their own
structure and law. Each human embryo proves his kinship to
fish and beast. Man's blood is still salt from the sea; the hackles
still rise along his spine.

No man is an island, nor is mankind a continent of itself. We are involved in all life, all geography, all energy. The charts of the seas and of the stars are as meaningful to us as the map of our own county, or the chart of our nerves and bones and veins, for sea and star are involved in our destiny, and we in theirs. There is no individual, no absolute individuality. We live by the grace of a universe that, as its name implies, is truly one.

But unless we practise, we cannot know this. Because we shirk the practice of oneness we are prisoned in self and cut off from the replenishing springs of life.

To reunite ourselves with the living stream of universal consciousness and creativeness is the function of meditation—an art which is natural to us but still must be learned. Like music, it comes from within our own nature, yet we must study attentively to create or to play it.

Where did Beethoven find the melodies of the slow movement of the Fifth Symphony, or Bach the endlessly rich spiritual outpouring of his choral preludes and Passions? They were not in the world before, but they are with us for as long as man endures. Meditation, too, is an art, spun out of that fertile flow of creativeness, that fountain of life, that lies within. The more we call upon it, the more we use it, the stronger it grows.

An art. "All things are artificial," wrote Sir Thomas Browne, "for nature is the art of God." Meditation is the art of man's nature, and his link with the divine. It is the word that mirrors the Word which was in the beginning. "And God said, Let there be light: and there was light." We, too, can speak the word which brings light. We can shine the light of the mind upon experience and see it clean.

Meditation unlocks the prison and loosens the chains of self. It restores us to our birthright of stream and storm and star. Its power waits like the current in the wire, ready to become light once the proper resistance is placed in its path.

In times of crisis—joy, sorrow, fear, anticipation—everyone

19

tries meditation, whether he knows it or not. Experience brims over, and instinct forces you to sip it up. But without practice beforehand, the rich draught spills and is lost.

"The brain is wider than the sky." That is the secret of meditation. We have only to stretch ourselves upon that wide arch and trust in it, as birds trust the air beneath their wings, as fish trust the depths of ocean, as our feet pretend the earth is still though it whirls through space.

Meditation, again, is not mere concentrated thought. It is a spectrum of human potentiality. In the act of meditating, the senses are at work as well as the mind. The body is quiescent but acute, as if it were the dynamo supplying power which runs through the veins and nerves as a live current, issuing in the mind as light.

Thus meditation is a creative act, not very different from writing poetry. It is an effort, by concentrating all the powers of the person, to harmonize the individual with the universal. Like poetry or religion or drama it must deal in symbols—the Word, light, grace, redemption. But its goal is heightened experience, perfected awareness.

BEGINNING

Meditation calls upon all of one's inner resources and exercises them. As physical exercise develops the muscles, or practice in mental arithmetic brings speed and accuracy, or the practice of surgery results in increased proficiency, so meditation develops alertness, responsiveness, understanding, sympathy, contentment, gratitude, inner peace. These things are not produced by riches, power, idleness or native talent. They come through what Jeremy Taylor called the practice of the presence of God.

Meditation calls upon resources we too often leave undeveloped—the power to be quiet, to empty the mind of its fantasies; to concentrate upon one thing and see into the heart of it, and through that one thing to find a mirror of the whole world and its unity, so that all becomes one, self merges with universe, "this is that."

Like this.

You wake in the morning and lie quietly, devoting ten minutes to meditation. If you find you cannot meditate lying down, get up and sit in a chair or in a Yoga position. (See page 116.) The important thing is to have the body at rest so that it does not intrude. There is a notion that one cannot or should not meditate lying down, but I can see no point to this so long as you are able to keep alert.

But what shall you meditate about?

It makes no difference. Start with the branch of a tree outside the window, the carved silhouette of the bedpost, the fresh air sweeping in, billowing the curtain as it comes, the mirror on the wall. Anything is good for meditation because whatever passes through the individual's mind becomes part of that individual and in this process of absorption the individual is extending his mastery of the art of merging not-self in self and self in all. (I don't mean to sound abstruse or vaporish, but this is the ground of meditation and we must get used to it.)

The mirror, then. If I should get up and look into it, what would I see? A middle-aged man with a sufficient number of furrows and wrinkles. And behind him some bits of a room endeared to him by the intimacies of wedded love. But what of the mirror itself? By what magic does it double the distance between me and it—measure out in precise geometry each detail it reflects, but then with a mischievous twist turn them backwards, so that it makes a mockery of print? A mockery of me, too—imitating every move I make.

Who or what determined these precise laws which every mirror must obey? How deep the mystery in the commonplace! I know little of the laws of optics, but I marvel at their iron rigidity, from the imperceptible speck viewed through a microscope to the behavior of starlight falling light-years through space. Not once in the world's history can one gleam of sunlight from a sun-struck lake, one glance of love or merriment in a mirror, one beam of starlight from outer space ignore or flout these laws. O Maker of law, how grand and wonderful is this creation! How strange a miracle that I should be a part of it, made safe from moment to moment by all these laws of light and weight and structure that operate in me and through me—through all the created world!

Yet I take all these things for granted, when, if I took a day to meditate about each of them, the span of my life would not be long enough to deal with them all.

What else does the mirror reflect? It shows me my skin and features. But this is not all. Why does it double the distance between us? Not only to wipe out in mercy some of my wrinkles, but to tell me perhaps that I must learn to stand back from myself in order to look dispassionately upon my faults. I must meditate upon these, one by one, day by day, and see what improvement I can make.

It speaks to me of the value of perspective in life. Would that I could set my problems in their proper framework as effortlessly as this piece of silvered glass surveys a whole room and catches every detail in right proportion, but in reverse so that we have a fresh view of it. A good plan to follow.

The mirror gives back an image of me. What image do I give back, to the ones I love, to those I work with, to the world? The mirror gives back an impartial image of whatever passes before it. Too often I do the same—giving back anger for anger, a mean answer for an ill-tempered one. Let me try the mirror trick of reversal. Let me give back mildness for anger, kindness for ill temper, love for hate. That way, if all of us studied our mirrors, we might remake a world.

"So God created man in his own image, in the image of God created he him."

Is that the image I give to the world? Am I a proper mirror for my creator?

I must get up now. But let me see if I can carry this with me through the day. Let me see whether the divine life that flows through me cannot shine as bright as that mirror, and keep its neat perspectives along with its bold—yes, and humorous—reversals, and be mindful of the joy and wonder of being, wherever I walk, a mirror for God.

BENEFITS OF MEDITATION

I hope this clarifies the point that you can make a meditation out of anything. I hope it also illustrates the point that meditation inevitably joins inner resources with some felt, larger unity. Once you feel that marriage, and repeat it daily with all the infinite variety the mind can find in daily experience, meditation will enlarge your life, your world.

Meditation strengthens the power to use all our inner resources —memory, the senses, the response to symmetry, rhythm, poetry, music, the power to perceive similarities in widely different fields, a sensitiveness to people and their qualities.

It does more than this. It draws all perceptions together in a total experience. This is the quality that will be lacking in every example I give of a meditation—the quality of the experience itself as it feels inside the experiencer. So my examples are only pale symbols of the real thing—the rose without the scent, the music as it looks on the page rather than as it comes from the orchestra, the photograph of the lovely girl rather than her living presence. Meditation is not words—it is experience. Let us not forget that.

So we can say that meditation, rightly and continuously practised, will bring relief from tension and anxiety, a sense of new power, a sense of participation in that creative energy which is both the symbol and the reality of the divine, and a sense of being at one with the great mystics who have caught this vision. We can say it, but the meditator will feel it. We may be stirred to this feeling by words, by music, by birdsong or sunrise or silence. But feel it we must.

2

THE STARTING GATE

To each his own, in meditation as in thumbprint, speaking voice, and love. There are as many ways in meditation as there are minds to meditate, and every seeker must explore and develop his own. The important point is to keep seeking, keep experimenting until you find ways that are congenial. Then keep up the adventure by trying something else.

The main difficulty in meditation is getting started. The second is keeping on some kind of track so that you do not wander off into reverie. The third is rounding the meditation so that it has some point and conclusion.

Yet starting is really not difficult, for one can start anywhere and with anything—even with a single word. And even this beginning has many variations.

1. You might take a word like love, joy or peace and repeat it until its meaning takes hold of you and lifts you. Or take any simple word—"bargain," for instance. Listen to it in your mind. "Bar gain." Ah, so that's what it means. I was in my middle years before I made that simple discovery, so obtuse are we to the obvious meanings in words as in life. The etymology is not as clear as common sense would suggest, but no matter—we are not etymologists now. To bar gain—what is the ethics of that? Does it mean that the merchant who advertises bargains is hurting other merchants? Is he selling something which misfortune has forced another man to sell at a loss? Has the laborer

lost his due wage in producing it? Or do bargains, by stimulating trade, help everybody by making more employment, by bringing the cost of goods within the reach of all? What is the ethics of gain, anyway? How much is it fair for a man to profit—in the work of his own hands, on items which he merely passes from maker or wholesaler to user, on services he renders others? How does society determine these rewards? Is our society fair and rational in the way it rewards carpenters, teachers, actors, prize fighters, hospital employees, doctors? Well, this is enough to suggest where a word can lead.

2. But you might prefer merely to repeat a word. Repeat your name. Somehow this has a strange, mesmeric effect. It seems to objectify the self, so that you are as if in a tree looking down upon the other you. From this point you may go in many directions—to self-analysis, a strengthening resolve, or to a memory of the you that is past—the time you fell downstairs, or first rode a bicycle, or got your first dog or your first girl friend.

3. Or you may take any word that comes into your head and repeat it without conscious purpose or aim: Valley. Valley. Valley, valley, valley.

How green was my valley. . . . Yea, though I walk through the valley of the shadow of death. . . . The valley of death. But first comes the valley of life. And have I walked it with my eyes open, my lungs full of its bracing air? Every valley shall be exalted. What does that mean? By its fruits, I think. And what are mine? There is no valley without hills. I have climbed them, and I shall climb again. I will lift up mine eyes unto the hills. But it is good to walk in the valley, beside the still waters. From whence cometh my help? My help cometh from the Lord, who hath made heaven and earth.

Hill and valley and still water, mountain and canyon and deep are the work of one creation; and why have I been placed in it? And what do I do in it, with such a little while before I am gone? The valley stays, and the hills I climb now, and the still waters run, and I will be laid somewhere beneath them all. Yet in time they, too, will be gathered up in some mighty motion of fire or flood or ice. Therefore all valleys are shadowed with death, yet they live in beauty. And the shadow, as in painting, is what gives roundness and ripeness to shapes and colors that would otherwise have little beauty at all. Death rims life with the beauty of transiency. It is because beauty is always passing—clouds moving, waters flowing, leaves scattering, youth aging—that it so pierces our hearts. The valley of life is shadowed with death, but this is my valley and I will live at peace in it.

4. Another way to work from a word would be to look one up at random in an unabridged dictionary to see what its connections are. If you look up "wit," for example, you will find that it goes back to the Sanskrit root *vid,* to know (Veda = knowledge) or to find, and that it is related to many other words —history, idea, idol, vision, wise, wisdom. So this might set off another train of thought. Wit is both wisdom and vision. Knowing is finding. The idea becomes our idol, and all enters into history, becomes history. Give me the wit, O divine source, to seek and to find; the wisdom to know when I have found; the vision to know what I have found and what remains yet to find.

Starting from the dictionary, however, may be dangerous if you love dictionaries, for meditation might get lost in pedantry, in information for its own sake. So beware!

Another way of using words is to make an acrostic. LIFE, for example, combines Love with Intelligence, Fun with an itch for Enlightenment.

5. Questions also provide good starting points for meditation. A question, by its nature, leads on to something else—often to other questions, to perplexity, possibly to an answer. The trick is to know how to ask the right questions.

What is man? Science could give us the chemical content and a quotation as to the market value of the chemicals. It used to be about eighty-seven cents, but inflation has no doubt trebled that. The Psalmist improved on the question by asking, What is man that thou art mindful of him? And after an initial cheapening, ended by placing him little lower than the angels.

Suppose we ask, Who is man? Well, who is he? The cousin of apes or the son of God? A stage in the evolutionary process from primal ooze to superman or a being unique in cosmic history? The dweller in Plato's cave, or the seer of divine visions? The inventer of war or the prince of peace? Al Capone or Walt Whitman? Jesus or Judas?

This is only a beginning.

6. Another way of using questions is to return to the whys of children. Why is water wet? Why do I have to go to sleep? Where does the wind come from? Why do the leaves whisper?

It is said that children, when they ask these questions, are not seeking a scientific explanation, but merely reassurance that what they see is so. They are learning to verify their senses by checking with another observer.

It would be good for us, instead of taking for granted the wetness of water, the refreshment of sleep, the joy of fresh air, and the pleasures of sight and smell and sound, to regard them afresh with child eyes and to see the miracle in them. That is how these questions might be used.

7. Or we might invent questions that shock the mind to new awareness with their radical departures. What is the color of love? How late is infinity? Who paints the sky? What puddle best mirrors the sky? What tune expresses dawn? What is the smell of purple? How high is the sky? What song does the moon sing? What would be the nature of a rose growing from a pine tree? The difference between a jazz hymn and religious jazz?

8. A variation on the radical question would be to propose implausibles to the mind. God interviews a murderer. A prostitute preaches a sermon. A world moratorium on violence. The scientist is asked to prove that God does not exist. Let me think like a woman—or, if a woman, like a man.

9. Or let us meditate the impossible: Warm snow. Dry rain. Wet desert. A hunger of repletion. An illumined darkness. Silent music. A smell with sharp edges. A medical cure for stealing, killing, anger, jealousy or hate. Full knowledge and wisdom suddenly infused into us electronically. A world swept clean for a new start, and the specifications we would write for it.

10. Begin with a poem you are fond of, or a melody you find moving. Say the poem through in your mind, then go back and listen to each line, seeking new meanings and the secret of its magic. Listen to the melody and ask yourself why it has the power to move you. Is it because of association with the past? Because it suggests some natural beauty? Because it induces a mood of calm or joy or longing or elation? In the poem or in the melody some central meaning, something deeply significant to you, is bound to be seated. Find it, and meditate upon that.

11. Make a song or a poem of your own. Never mind about its imperfections; spin it out of yourself, and let it go where it will. Come back and try to repeat it. But don't worry about preserving it.

12. Everyone, at some time or other, has the experience of entering into something else and becoming part of a scene, a group, a painting, a silence. Empathy, the psychologists call it.

You look out upon a well-loved scene, and suddenly it is as if the mountains draw you out through the window and take you to themselves, while at the same time the mountains seem to be drawn in through your eyes and into the center of your being. It is a good starting point for meditation. What is the source of this oneness? How and why do I feel it? Why do I lift up my eyes unto the hills, and what is the nature of the strength I find there? Or, of course, one may simply concentrate upon the experience without speculating on it. This sort of meditative activity will be dealt with later, in the chapter on Mysticism.

Or you are sitting, perhaps in your own living room, with a group of friends. A sense of warmth and enrichment flushes your body like the warming of wine (which many godly men have accepted as a godly gift), and you sense yourself as a part of the group almost as if you were all one body. What significance does this have for the human group, and for each of its members? How might you nourish and foster that warmth where it is needed —in community relations, in church or parent association or neighborhood? What is the source of this oneness you share with others? Could it be nourished in groups where hostility prevents proper functioning? By what means?

13. One of the easiest doorways to meditation is through the miracles that lie all about us—the growth of spring, a flower opening, a sunset, bees working, the dart and hover of a hummingbird.

14. But for the temper that is mathematical, scientific or statistical, the way of wonder may seem unattractive. Science will do equally well.

Science and the kind of religion we are concerned with in this book are at one in basing themselves upon experience. Both are experimental, both sensitive to perception, in receptiveness to what is new and in eagerness to examine and value it without bias, in refining distinctions and understanding differences, in insisting upon an integrity which will not report what cannot be verified and will not reject what fails to fit a preconceived theory, in ability to grapple with the abstract, in faith in the natural world and the reliability of universal laws which work at all times and at all places, and therefore in the astounding idea of a universe—an incredibly intricate organism every part of which fits into a whole, whose parts and whose whole, whose laws and motions are susceptible of being perceived, probed and understood.

Without this faith in universals, which the scientist takes so much for granted that he hardly thinks of it, scientific inquiry would be impossible.

But it is still a mysterious universe we live in. Science does not dispel the mystery; every new discovery merely deepens it. True religion has nothing to fear from science, for every scientific discovery necessarily becomes another tribute to the mind of the maker. The more science reveals the tremendous complexity of life and nature and its essential unity, the deeper grows the mystery.

Faith is not blind. Its eye is the mind. The mind is the only instrument we have for the investigation of reality. Microscopes, computers, telescopes, space capsules—all are but devices for making that one instrument more sensitive. But when all this work is done, there is still more to do. Science tells us how, but not why. To pursue this question we must use the same instrument the scientist uses, but microscopes and telescopes are no help to us here. We must refine the basic instrument—the mind.

As it is the mystery of being which stimulates the true scientist to explore the world of nature or of man, so the continuing sense of that mystery will stimulate speculation on the origin of life and the nature of the law that determines all laws. "Euclid alone has looked on Beauty bare." The mind that is drawn toward science will be strengthened by exploring the why as well as the how. This is a way of meditation that may even be helpful to science.

A scientist who can enter into his problem and see it as if he were the maker of the law on which it is based is likely to solve his problems more quickly than the man who sees only the mechanics. The great discoveries in science have combined hard work with inspired hunches.

Even those of us not learned in science can gain from thinking about the great speculations of Galileo, Newton, or Einstein, and the gradual unfolding of an even more wonderful universe through their work.

A look through a microscope has the quality of revelation the first time, opening up a world that ever after is a part of an enlarged experience. So also with the telescope. All these enlarged perceptions provide material for meditation.

15. Memory is a broad stairway leading to meditation. To let the mind select some scene or event out of the past and then focus on it is a good way of beginning. The way memory will preserve some events—even apparently unimportant ones— while disposing of others is a mystery. But every event that is remembered must have significance. Often we remember only the detail, and delight in it because it so magically recaptures the past and makes it live. We enjoy (or suffer) the event without perceiving its significance.

Meditation can search out the significance and give new value to the memory.

I am twelve years old and in the eighth grade. I am small for my age, and at least a year younger than my classmates. They have gone into long pants, and I am still wearing mine at the knees, with black cotton stockings to bridge the gap between shoe top and breeches.

But at last the day comes, and on a Sunday morning I climb the stairs to the second floor of the Parish House, both elated and terribly embarrassed, and Helen—the belle of our age group —turns in the doorway and looks at me as I come up and says, "Oh, look at Brad—he's got long pants."

The embarrassment was excruciating—I was a shy child anyway. No boy nowadays has to suffer this symbolic leap from child to man. But I did, and I remember it still—both the cruel exposure and the sweet achievement.

Perhaps it's obvious enough why I remember this. But the experience opens the way to meditation in many directions— the changes that have taken place in our informalized society, the nature of *rites du passage* which mark the youngster's arrival at manhood, the ages of man, and the combined sense of exhilaration and heartbreak with which one moves on from one to the next.

In some such way every memory contains a meditation.

16. Begin with a person. Since childhood impressions are so often stronger than those of maturity, it might be more effective to take first a person who meant a great deal to you in childhood. Perhaps a grandmother, an uncle, a teacher, or your closest friend. The miracle of memory can bring this person back as if he, or she, were standing at your shoulder. The past will live again as you hear the voice, catch the smile, recall a scene in every detail of light and color and sound.

Think continuously of the person—of what he, or she, meant to you and in what manner you have been strengthened by this relationship, and could be further if you would thus think of all the friends and relatives whose love and trust has built a wall of strength for you. They dwell in you; their strength fortifies you and even their foibles guide and warn you. Stored and hidden in your memory are hundreds of people, each of whom through meditation can strengthen what you are or what you want to be.

Or you might start with a person you dislike. Walk around him in your mind. See how he eats, talks, smiles, promises, performs. How does he behave towards his wife, towards children, towards employees or those who serve him, and towards those whose regard he values? What stands does he take on public issues? What does he do in and for the community? What is the source of your dislike? How would he be different if you were acting for him? Are the things you dislike in him faults you can also find in yourself? Often we hate most in others the things we subconsciously recognize as failures or potential weaknesses in ourselves. To think about someone you dislike may therefore be the best way to trick yourself into a realization of your own fault, and thus to amend it.

17. When you catch yourself in a bad mood, enter upon a brief meditation wherever you are. Ask: Why am I blue, or angry, or sad, or fearful? Confront the difficulty. Analyze it. Regard it in the light of eternity. Search your mind for an idea which will lift you above the mood. Then experience the joy of that

33

power within by which you are able to lift yourself, and the sense of the inward divinity which is helping you.

18. Each morning, lie still when you wake up, searching your sleep for dreams that may clarify your fears and hopes and plans. Then sense the restful repose of your body in the moment before you begin an active day. Then establish contact with the inward light which will guide you through the day's work. Then look with anticipation towards tasks, relationships with friends and colleagues, and pleasures of work and play the day holds for you. If you are having difficulty with an employee or a boss, try to see his personality as if from within him, and search for what in you irritates him and vice versa.

19. Each night as you relax in bed, think over the irritations, the joys and the discoveries of the day. Sense them gratefully, and ask yourself what is to be learned from them.

20. Think: "I am that bird soaring. I am that light shining. I am those leaves turning in the wind. I am that mountain firmly, calmly enduring. I am Socrates. I am the patient near death with cancer. I am that child, full of wonder. I am that old man, full of peace and acceptance and grace. I am myself, which is all that I can imagine or comprehend or reach towards—and also that which I cannot reach.

"I am all that has entered into me from the beginning of time, for all time is in me and all futurity. I am the mother who gave me birth, the father whose seed fertilized me, the teachers who taught me, the friends who companioned and corrected me. I am my children and their children; I am my ancestors and all that unknown life which went into me before man was. I am all that I hear, smell, see and think. And what I am not, I am hitched to by my human, animal, cellular, divine nature. God grows inwardly, and I grow outward from that inwardness, and somehow we are perfectly joined."

21. In the act of love, I recognize in sexual ecstasy the one

ground which unites all men and women of all ages and cultures, making of them one race, one kind, binding them in one uniting, creative experience.

22. Walk outside in the early morning and, if you are lucky enough to live where there is earth, look into the face of a flower. What is the source of this perfect designing, and what is the function of this beauty of color and form?

23. If you have a pain or an ache, meditate upon its meaning. Why pain? Suppose there were no pain, as in the rotting flesh of a leper? Why is absence of pain a sign of incompleteness? How do we distinguish pain from pleasure in the overbearingness of passion, in the tired muscles after sport? What can we learn from pain that we do not learn from pleasure?

24. Teach yourself to hold one-minute meditations when you would otherwise be wasting time—before meals, while washing, driving, going up or down in an elevator.

LOOKING IN AND UP

A meditation might begin in a hundred other ways, but these twenty-four, with all their variations, are enough to launch anyone into the habit of daily exercise in this art. Try reading just one of them again, then close the book and let your mind work on it. Each suggestion in this book can be used that way, one at a time.

But meditation does not stop with a purely logical mulling over of a past or present scene or impression. Meditation always aims at nesting the individual in the universe. It goes beyond logic. It calls upon inner powers and insights that get choked off by our daily routine. Much of what follows in this book will deal with that higher range of meditation, but we need to be aware of it in the beginning too.

In Yoga a good deal is made of posture. But at the beginning we can be content with any posture which encourages both comfort and awareness, so that the body can be ignored and the mind enlarged.

As you settle yourself and, as the Quakers put it, "center down," you may discover a very simple principle. You will find yourself looking either down or up, and the direction in which you look will either reflect or modify the nature of your meditation.

It makes no difference whether your eyes are open or shut. I find it helpful to keep mine closed; this helps me to concentrate on the inwardness of the experience. In Zen meditation the eyes are kept half-closed to emphasize the balance between inner and outer worlds. Some Yoga exercises involve staring at a candle flame or some other point of light.

With eyes closed and head lowered, you will find yourself concentrating inward, perhaps in one of the ways suggested in the foregoing pages. If the meditation is successful (and we are anticipating here, for much yet remains to be said and experienced about the spiritual illumination that comes from within), you will begin to feel peace and acceptance and certainty spreading over you like a warm blanket. When you have completed the first phase of the meditation—recalling a person or a poem or entering into a beloved scene—you should find yourself floating upon it as on a raft. It bears you up, as the quiet waters bear the raft of your being. This unit of experience is your support upon the deep waters of a consciousness which merges into all experience, all consciousness, all being.

In this situation, looking down and in, and having found there one out of a million items which demonstrates and establishes the authenticity of the inner person, you will sooner or later feel the spirit of it taking hold of you. Wait in quietness and it will come—the sense of an inner wealth stored up in the brain like honey in the cells of a hive: a rich, sweet food to be drawn upon at need.

The feeling may report itself first as warmth or fullness, then as well-being or joy; in any case, a presence. It is this presence, this sense of presence which must be cultivated and nurtured until it fills all of life.

To some it may be immediately accepted as a spiritual, a divine presence. If so, good; if not, never mind.

At the point when this happens, it is very likely that you will unconsciously raise your head. Light from a window or a lamp falling on the closed eyes will often create an arousing effect of illumination that is more than physical. To the religious it will seem like the light that blinded Paul on the road to Damascus, a joyous cascade of radiance shedding itself upon the world of men, entering the heart and drenching the soul.

The two postures—down and in, out and up—illustrate the two aspects of divinity as it has reported itself to man's receptive sensibilities through the centuries: immanence and transcendence. There is no conflict between them, though theologians have sometimes made conflict where none exists. The instinct which teaches us to look down and in, then out and up, demonstrates that something within us turns naturally to these two sources of illumination. Together they make a completed radiance in which we recognize the divine.

"For God, who commanded the light to shine out of darkness, hath shined in our hearts." In this beautiful phrase, Paul (II Corinthians 4:6) has simply and eloquently brought transcendence and immanence together.

It may be apparent by now that I have stepped warily out of deference to those who are irritated by religious terminology or who may feel that they are complete atheists. Meditation is for everyone, atheist or believer, and I have tried to speak to every condition. But at this point it has to be said that meditation will not take a person very far if he cannot respond to that which is greater than human, and better. I do not really believe there are such people, but so many have been put off by orthodoxies no longer tenable and by childish renderings of the divine nature that they think themselves atheists. They have their place. The divine All must include the idea of no-god as well as God.

From now on, I shall use the words "divine," "God," and "spirit" in the hope that each reader will define them for himself and in answer to his own need and conviction, but will not in any case press them into a strait jacket of some definition carried over from childhood.

Why does the idea of God keep recurring to men's minds in all times, places and seasons? "Thou wouldst not seek Me if thou hadst not already found Me," says Pascal, and with this beautiful phrase dissolves all those meaningless mountains of theological controversy. It is that God—whose already implied presence is in the search—who comes into meditation.

A TYPICAL MEDITATIVE CYCLE

Every meditation will be different from every other, thanks to the wonderful richness of the human consciousness and the possibility of variety within the encompassing oneness. Yet, as an illustration of what one may expect, it may be worth while to describe a typical meditative cycle.

I enter my room, shut the door, get comfortably seated, let my head drop naturally and close my eyes. Breathing is quiet, the body relaxed. I wait in silence, not forcing anything, not hurried, but sensitive to what the mind may turn up.

Unbidden, a memory of my grandmother sitting at her big window sewing comes sharply into focus. I recall her spacious, gracious house, and the family Thanksgivings we had there. Other scenes, people, recollections, rise to surround her. I hold each in my mind and turn it, searching for what is significant. I work all this like a cud, or like paints on a palette. Gradually everything begins to assume shape and order—the memories, the details, the sensations, and the ideas. They form a pattern or a design in my mind. My grandmother remains the central figure, as she was the central figure of her family, and as her home symbolized for us a family solidarity that included not only sisters, cousins and aunts but the great-grandfather I never knew who had owned a good part of the town, and who slept in the cemetery lot we decorated every Memorial Day. And beyond him, by the family tree, to Plymouth. And beyond that? To England, of course. But thereafter? What is the meaning of this cycle of life, sensed so strongly in those we knew who in their turn go to the lot and are visited on Memorial Day, but also reaching deep into the past and carrying us with it?

All this lives in me, a reality and a mystery. For me, my grandmother still sits as visibly in her chair by the window as she did twenty or thirty years ago. And her love still warms me. Somewhere in the mystery of love the whole riddle of personality and inheritance and continuity is hidden.

I must relax now—not strain at the thought, for straining will strangle it—and let all this matter flow past again in a new form and order, suffused with the glow of recollection (the family faces around the Thanksgiving dinner table, the hush, the prayer, the bustle, the repletion, the collapse on the parlor sofa) until it takes on a form of its own and becomes a new experience. Perhaps it is a sudden realization of the unity we all had as a family, now so scattered and never after grandmother's death to be together again except as now in this meditation. Or perhaps it is the sweet sadness of the passage of time, or the onetime deep affection for cousins who have now grown up and become strangers.

All this now flows from the verbal into a deeper, nonverbal level where it is felt as warmth, as youth returning, as the dead revivified, as a unity recaptured and savored and preserved.

And now, as with music ended, I sink back into quietness—relaxed, resting in the bed of these memories, dissolved into the unity with life stretching backward beyond my sight and for-

light in the branches / rain-wet trees!

ward to the unknown. I am the center of this life because I think myself to the center, and so is everyone else who will think his way there. Each life is a cycle, but one that turns within the millions of other orbits to which it belongs, as a single proton is related not only to its own nucleus but to all the other atoms in its neighborhood and to the molecule they form and the material they make up, and by their behavior to every other atom in the universe. In the same way—no, in a far higher way—I am involved in mankind. And the involvement is God, for that involvement involves a mind—or a way, or a law—which surpasses human capacity.

So, in the end of my meditation, I have come to a sensing, far deeper than the words I have used to express it, of the oneness which overtakes the searcher and gathers him up.

BENEFITS AND REWARDS

I have tried to give an actual rather than an ideal instance of the way a meditation might go. The important point is that any starting point will do, because if the search is honestly pursued it will lead to a finding. "Seek, and ye shall find; knock, and it shall be opened unto you." (Matthew 7:7.)

It should also be apparent that with any success at all a meditation will convert stray thoughts to esthetic form, will bring order out of a random scattering of memories and impressions. And this is a function of the mind which demonstrates its divinity: the compelling thirst for order, for form, for beauty. Where does such a compulsion come from? However the explanation is phrased, it can only assume a superior mind which has made order in the universe and to which the human mind vibrates, as if a great string had been plucked to which our minds and hearts must respond.

A meditation is a work of art, a point to which we shall return in a later chapter. It works with any material that comes to hand, shaping it by an instinct whose source is our unity to a form that satisfies, enlightens and invigorates. Meditation is not only about something: it is experience transforming the individual through a working art into a divine instance of the Divine.

Those who like method and order may want to keep a note-book of meditations, in which the significant beginning thought and the main developing ideas are noted. Others will prefer to keep no record, finding that the nonverbal part of meditation, which could never be set down, is the more valuable. An advantage of the book might be that one could discover something about his own patterns of thought, detect themes that repeat themselves, and delve deeper with them until the way opens to a profounder level of challenge and response than had ever seemed possible.

Most people have shallow thoughts because they are afraid of deeper ones. They fear to challenge the idea of God, of family, of nation, of brotherhood, of success, and of failure—which various social pressures are always making them accept and conform to. It is as if all these pressures kept them pinned against a wall so that they could never look up or sidewise or down.

Meditation honestly pursued will free you from all that. Alone in the quiet fifteen minutes to half an hour which you give to yourself each day for the things that really matter, you can confront all these without fear, and with the exhilarating prospect of learning what you truly think and thinking what you truly know, deepening as you go.

In meditation you can free yourself from the trammels that bind you in your daily life. Progressively you will be able to transfer your findings into living, until what confronts you there can be fearlessly dealt with in your time of meditation. The meditative habit will gradually work over into all activity. You will learn to evaluate as you go, to drop or severely limit activities that are meaningless, and to shape your life so that it conforms to the divinity that is within.

41

Meditation: The Inward Art

Then you will see that meditation is the truly active element in life, the gyroscope that keeps you in balance, an individual afloat in a universe that is either a hostile ocean or a mothering element, depending on how you adjust yourself to it. Meditation will become a habit, replacing the hasty, thoughtless decisions and passions by which most lives are governed. It will go like a shadow alongside all other activity, so that all experience comes to have meaning—a meaning which is constantly being plumbed and recorded and fed back into the stream of life to deepen it.

Meditation is a form of doing, a way of working. Its results should be seen in deeper awareness, fuller response, wiser decisions, more balanced living, clearer definition of goals and more success in reaching them. And in a feeling of knowing who you are and what you are about, as well as a sense of having expanded out of the narrow self into a world of which you are a working part. And in a mood of serenity and joy. Having learned to look at yourself as if you were someone else, you should also have learned to look at others as if they were yourself.

But beyond all this, meditation like music is an end in itself. It demands the best of those human qualities which because they are human are most like the divine. You meditate just as you play a violin or make love or write a poem or make a garden—out of a hunger for oneness, out of a desire to merge self with all, out of faith that what you feel in yourself will find a response in others, out of hope that there is indeed a bridge from the human to the divine.

3

WAYS OF MEDITATING

HAVING suggested a few start-
ing points, and having described a meditative experience, I can
now risk being a little more didactic. But I do not want to imply
that meditation should cling to iron rules. All that follows is
mere suggestion. Meditation is a creative experience, not a routine.

The first need is for silence. But silence has many forms. There
is the silence of deep woods, the silence of a church, of an empty
office building at midnight, of a house when all have gone to
bed, of a morgue, a dissecting room in a medical school, an
early morning in a boat in the middle of a lake, or between enemies or friends, or in the moment after an accident before the
scream rises, or the silence of pain or despair or sleep or after-
math of love.

Silence is not dead; each silence has its own rhythm and pulsa-
tion.

"Be still, and know that I am God."

This is the ground of meditation—the silence into which a divine presence can enter.

"The Lord is in his holy temple: let all the earth keep silence
before him." (Habakkuk 2:20.)

The silence of meditation is a holy silence. It is also dynamic.
For when the mind has emptied itself of the daily turmoil and
begun to float serene upon the current of silence, another current slowly begins to assert itself. At first it may be like the waves

which turn backward on themselves in a tumbling stream. But as it grows, establishes and asserts itself it is like a boat borne upon the stream and sunk part way within it. This is the current of thoughts crystallized in words. The stream bears the vessel, but is not the vessel. The vessel could not travel without the stream. A dynamic union and tension exists between them.

To shift the metaphor, they are like two birds flying together, sometimes close, sometimes separating, but aware of each other, dependent. Or like two voices singing in counterpoint.

In this working tension, silence bears upon its stream the flow of thoughts which grow into unspoken words. (Those who can retire to a private place may even find it helpful to speak or whisper the words that make thought tangible.) Silence exerts itself to grow beyond its nature into words; words rise to the surface and sink back into silence. Of this dynamic tension meditation is born.

If the meditation is successful, it will raise out of the stream of silence a stream of thoughts which concentrate and become meaningful, and which end by drawing together things experienced, or known, or thought, into a pattern of new significance. Meditation discovers the truth that lies hidden in experience. It discovers the relationships between nature, human and divine.

It must deal with words, for words are the symbols by which we grasp ideas. In the act of using words, however, we should be aware of their limitations. Language is analytical—it breaks things up into separate parts. There is danger in this. Words restrict and falsify as easily as they disclose and clarify. We talk of economic, political, social, psychological, as if these were separate entities when they are only aspects of human behavior. Then we also forget that they are but conceptual distinctions, and regard them as having validity by themselves. Reality is a continuum, not a shopping list of separate items.

In everyday problem-solving thought we have to pretend that

44

these separate categories are real. The policeman pretends that arresting a man for breaking into the shop and hauling him before the judge disposes of the matter, yet all our social shortcomings and failures are involved in this event. The chemist pretends that the reaction he brings about in his flask has no relation to the geological sources of his material or a possible biological effect of its use. The physician diagnoses an ailment and writes a prescription on the assumption that the illness is an isolated phenomenon, although it may have been brought on by worry or poor eating habits.

We go through life re-enacting what I call the analytic fallacy. Meditation restores the balance. It sees that life is one.

Silence is a deeper thing than quiet, but we need quiet too, both within and without. Thanks to TV, radio, the internal combustion motor, and a few other blessings of modern life, quiet is hard to come by. But it is worth seeking, whether in bedroom or forest, in a library or in a rowboat in the middle of a still lake. In time, meditation will also become possible in a subway, a plane, or a car—or perhaps even when the rest of the family is intent upon TV.

Let us assume a quiet room. You take a chair that is comfortable but firm, sit in it with your back firmly supported and find a position you can hold without undue squirming and shifting.

Relax. Relax all the muscles, consciously and methodically, from head to foot. Take pleasure in this relaxing; enjoy it. If there was tension, let it flow out at your finger tips. Close your eyes. Let your head drop to a position that is natural and comfortable. Breathe a few deep breaths, filling your lungs and letting the air out slowly, then let your breathing become quiet and natural. Now try to forget your body; let it take care of itself, let it be quiet and at ease.

Now let the mind run freely for a bit. It will pick up and examine an odd assortment of things—a job unfinished, a surly

45

face, a gracious response, a memory from the past that seems completely unrelated. The purpose is to let the mind run down until it, too, is quiet.

There are many ways to proceed from here on. If an idea comes into the mind that seems to have possibilities, hold it and explore around it. Almost anything will serve—a face, a scene, a book or article recently read.

Or you may simply raise your head so that light from a window or lamp will flood your closed eyes. Let the light flood inward until it seems to flow into the brain and lighten the mind, bringing a sense of buoyancy and illumination and peace. Let this feeling establish itself until it is there within you, with a certainty of warmth and well-being.

If you prefer a more specific regimen, try this:

1. Start with a few breathing exercises (see pages 111–12).
2. Sit and grow calm.
3. Make yourself one with

> nature—sun, air, plants, water;
> sentient beings—dog dozing, bird flying;
> people—wife, children, colleagues, friends;
> self.

4. Think about a desired virtue. Who that you know has it? Who in history had it most perfectly? How can you practise to acquire or strengthen it?

5. Think about a disliked fault. Observe it in others and how it affects those around them. Then switch it so that you see this same fault in yourself and its effect on others. What is its opposite virtue? How is that to be acquired?

6. Place an upcoming problem of the day before your mind. Then wait patiently without forcing it, and see what suggestions will come. See it as if it were someone else's problem, and you were trying to advise them how to handle it.

7. Merge yourself with others who are concerned in the problem. Consider how many others face a similar problem. Visualize

46

its universal aspects. Then bend it back into yourself and deal with it as if it were universal.

Or if your bent is more reflective and philosophical, try this discipline for meditation:

First, of being. Let the mind drift relaxed, and when a word, a thought, a tune, an image, comes that seems fruitful, hold it and let it grow. (*Example:* I hear a tranquil phrase of Beethoven and speculate on its meaning—the harmony of man with nature, why man conceived music, the urge to self-expression, self-realization.)

Second, of self. Self-expression is creative; self-understanding, critical; self-realization results from a dialogue of the critical and the creative. If I would strengthen myself, I must first understand myself. What are my strengths, and how shall I best use them? My weaknesses, and how shall I overcome them? Let me look at each of these weaknesses, one by one, as if they were another's. Then look at the weaknesses in others that irritate me and see if they are not also in me. Then let me see how with my strengths I can overcome my weaknesses. (*Example:* I love children but am impatient with adults. Let me learn to see the child that is in every adult, and have patience with that.)

Third, of the past. The past is a deep forest in which I wander at will. In it I find a spring of fresh water, and silence, and sweet odors, and a breeze that stirs the branches. It is enough for one meditation to take one sip from the spring, one leaf from a single tree. (*Example:* Thinking of childhood, I recall the time when I was three or four, and stood on a sea wall with a girl named Martha White whom I have never seen since, and the sea wind blew her dark hair and her blue-and-white seersucker dress against cheek and limb, and so far as I know the thought of beauty then first occurred to me.)

Fourth, strengthened by the living past, *I face a problem.* It may be grief, or suffering, or anxiety—my own, or that of someone I cherish. How do I fit this to the framework of the divinity I am trying to nurture? (*Example:* The moment we suffer, we ask "Why?" Did we ask the why of all the health and joy that went before? Let us ask first why life has survived its incredible cataclysms in order to produce man at all. We live by miracle and take it for granted, but think ourselves abused on the rare occasions when the miracle fails or falters.)

Fifth, I turn toward others. Beginning, perhaps, with one friend, I look at him both with love and with apartness and try to understand his uniqueness and my relation to him. Then my relations to others—particularly where I have failed. Then to the groups I belong to—family, church, professional organization, community, and to the universal brotherhood of man.

Sixth, the future. I shall think of ways in which my life might grow richer and fuller, enriching the lives of others. (*Example:* Suppose I had a year which I could free of ordinary business to devote to some urgent problem. What would it be? Where would I go? What would I do?)

Seventh, praise and adoration. Let us not be embarrassed by these words. "This is my God, and I will praise him." Noble words, ennobling to man if he can rise to them. But what God? What if his name still embarrasses me? What if I have no image of him? Begin then with what you love—your child, a piece of music, birdsong, the quiet night. Or love itself, pulsing and throbbing at the peak. We might begin this way:

> Lord of the universe, we adore thee—
> Breath in the breeze,
> Passion in the storm,
> Lord of the many voices—birdsong and water lapping
>   and the voice of woman,
> Life that leaps green out of dead grasses, leaves that
>   burst, and infants born of blood and tears in the
>   night,
> Lord of the law of love and death and thunder,

Lord of the law of light and flight and wonder—
Lord of the universe, we adore thee.

Eighth, a gathering in. I try now to see myself both inwardly and outwardly—in all the faults and in the few virtues I have located, in my relation to other individuals and groups, to nature, to concepts such as beauty, integrity and truth. There is matter for many meditations here, and we shall come later to types of meditation which try to shock the truth out of us. (*Example:* I have but one week to live. How shall I act and what shall I do? And should I not thus act and do now and forever, as if it were so?)

Ninth, realization. Drawing all these things together I see myself in time, in eternity, in childhood, in death, in the act of love, in anger and fear, in self-forgetfulness, in a trance of music, in danger, and at last in ecstasy—the meaning of it all summed up and brought out into the clear, like a symphony brought to its climax, its themes summed up, its instruments heard both separately and together, its meaning gathered to its end.

IN PRAISE OF ATHEISTS

Many good people avoid meditation because they fear what they might find. They want to believe, but social forces push them to a nominal faith they do not feel. What they hear, and what others seem to accept, strikes them as largely nonsense. So they go through the motions of Sunday worship, somewhat uncomfortable yet vaguely satisfied at having taken out at least that much fire insurance in case there is really a hell.

Better an honest atheist than a hypocrite, a pretending believer. There is more true religion in honest doubt than in dishonest orthodoxy. The doubter, the atheist has at least thought himself to his position; he has shown this much respect to religion.

Meditation: The Inward Art

The basis of meditation is honesty—honesty about ourselves, our beliefs, our goals. Here in the private chapel of internal solitude we face ourselves as we are. We do not pretend to be or believe anything that is not so. One way to promote this quality is to meditate on the theme:

There is no God.

What proof have I of the existence of God? Has he ever spoken to me, or to anyone I know? We read of him in old books. We know that he was real to Jesus, to the saints, to men like St. Augustine and St. Francis. But they lived before the scientific era. They could think of God as a person, a sort of super-father. Such an idea is unacceptable nowadays. We think in terms of force and energy, atomic structure and evolution. God didn't make man in his own image; man made God in his, and now that's not good enough. So we've lost God as a person, but what have we got in His place? You can't get steamed up religiously over atomic structure or the Van Allen belt or $E = mc^2$. Heaven is no longer on Olympus. God no longer speaks to Moses from the top of Mount Sinai.

So let's assume there is no God. Now we have to account for the amazing sense of plan, of mind, in the universe and all its phenomena. Why is matter made up mostly of energy—the material equivalent of "soul" or "spirit"? Why do the motions within the atom take their special courses? Granted we have a universe, incredible in its vastness and in the laws that hold it together, how is it that life came to exist on our own little planet, so inconspicuous a part of the whole? Were the laws of its development present before life was, in the beginning of the universe itself? Where and when was that beginning? What was before time was? What is the nature of eternity—a concept so beyond me that it reduces me to helpless laughter? How can I cope with the endlessness of space? Einstein has told us it is curved, but what does that really mean?

When I was a boy, I used to lie on the grass and look up into the depths of blue sky, and say to my companion, "What's up there?" "Space." "Beyond that?" "More space. It goes on forever." And we would stare upward, trying to pierce the mystery of foreverness but never succeeding.

How, then, can I explain to myself the existence of an ordered universe, bound together by implacable laws so weighty that they hold stars and suns in their courses and do not let them fall; so delicate that they keep every atom spinning within to a music which, if we could hear it, would no doubt sing like Shakespeare's stars:

> There's not the smallest orb which thou behold'st
> But in his motion like an angel sings,
> Still quiring to the young-eyed cherubins.
> —*The Merchant of Venice,* V, i.

How can I explain the miracle of soft new leaves emerging from brittle boughs, of a baby joining and repeating the traits of its parents or grandparents, of life-risking courage, and of cheerfulness in the face of disaster?

Is it not perhaps true that each man has his own god—whether power, or wealth, or joy, or pleasure, or belligerence, or beauty, or love? "For where your treasure is, there will your heart be also." (Matthew 6:21.)

What do I mean by God, anyway? Why do I fear the word or shy away from it? Is it because I think of Michelangelo's old whiskered gentleman? Or worse, of some stupid sermon or childish Sunday school lesson?

Let me substitute the word "divine." In its Sanskrit origin, "divine" meant radiant. God is the one who radiates—not a bad insight, suitable even to a scientific age. Surely we can perceive divinity—"radiance"—in the face of a child, the heart of a flower, the majesty of a storm, the melting strength of love.

51

Meditation: The Inward Art

My wife took some simple remedies to the ailing wife of our gardener in India, and soon the woman was cured. "Ah, she is a god," said the gardener of my wife. . . .

"Hinduism knows many gods, Christianity but one," a learned swami told me.

"Is it not strange that God should have favored one race of men above all others?" I asked.

"Perhaps it is because you do not recognize a god when he comes," said the swami. . . .

And Mr. Nehru said to me: "In India we think there is a bit of God in every man."

Quakers speak of the Inward Light or the divine seed or the Christ within, or "that of God in every man."

If it helps, let us think then of God as the radiance in face and flower and sun and star, in fire and frenzy and painting and symphony, in learning and wisdom and kindness and love.

God is man's poem of the good, his dream of the possible, his lust for perfection and his longing for immortality.

"The most beautiful thing we can experience," wrote Einstein, "is the mysterious. It is the source of all true art and science. . . . To know that what is impenetrable to us really exists, manifesting itself as the highest wisdom and the most radiant beauty which our dull faculties can comprehend only in their most primitive form—this knowledge, this feeling is at the center of religiousness."

Science, as it discovers universal law, only adds to the majesty and mystery of creation. Probing the mystery, as Einstein did, leads to man's greatest work. The probing may be by way of science, or poetry, or religion. All have something to say. If we had minds like that of the Creator, there would be no division between science and poetry and religion, for perfect knowledge would be whole. But we, with our shortcomings, must break it down. There is a danger then that we shall think of the scientific or the poetic or the religious explanation as the whole thing. Yet each is but a glimpse of reality, like looking out on a wide country-side through a crack in the door. For a full vision, we must try to put them together again; then the door will open upon reality in its true radiance.

This is what the Hindu does. "This is that." World soul and universal soul are one. As we probe the mystery and understand it better, we come closer to such a vision.

THE ONE AND THE MANY

Imagine two people sitting on opposite sides of a room, a vase of flowers between them on a table. Do they see the same thing?

Think of a concert hall full of people listening to one of the Brandenburg concertos of Bach. Do they all hear the same thing? Do they hear what the conductor hears? Or the first violins?

Two people stand at a window watching a sudden thunderstorm sweep down a valley. "How beautiful!" says one. "How horrible!" says the other.

The problem of unity and variety, of the one and the many, has plagued most men and all philosophers. The mind perceives both unity and variety, and yearns for both—even for both at once. We pride ourselves on our individuality, but ache to be merged into our social group—to be accepted, approved, loved. Yet the more we conform ourselves in order to be accepted, the more we lose the individuality which was the thing for which we craved acceptance.

See what happens when you meet a stranger, someone you think you might like to have for a friend. He makes a statement with which you don't agree. Instead of disagreeing amiably and honestly, you indicate a pale assent or make some noncommittal answer. No real friendship can grow on such a basis. If you had spoken your own convictions frankly, and yet with intellectual openness and humility, you might have established the basis for a firm and worthy friendship. Pale conformity leaches out the strengths that make sturdy human relations. The urge to unity stifles variety.

The problem crops up in every field. The philosopher may call it the one and the many. In esthetics it might be treated as theme and variations, repetition and innovation, unity and variety. The theologian might deal with monism and dualism or pluralism. In politics it appears as an attempt to satisfy both the freedom of many individuals and the need for consensus. In ethics it expresses itself as the right of the person as against his duty towards others and toward society. In religion it is the quest to merge the individual soul in the universal soul, or to experience both the divine presence within and the divine transcendence.

"A plurality is not to be admitted except by necessity," wrote William of Occam in the fourteenth century, and this has been the principle of science as well as religion. For it is a principle of science that a theory which can explain all relevant phenomena more simply will displace a more cumbrous one. Copernicus displaced Ptolemy. Galileo ultimately overcame those who insisted that the sun moves around the earth.

Both science and religion perceive that in the fertile variousness of life there is a unifying source. We once thought that every object in the material world consisted of unique particles each of which imparted its special shape or color or smell. Then came the discovery of chemical elements, which were thought to be immutable and unchangeable. Out of various combinations of elements such as hydrogen, oxygen and carbon all things were produced. Now we know that these elements have an inner life of their own, an atomic structure within which the component neutrons and protons establish their identity by their size and number and the nature of their movements. Each of these discoveries has tended to take us further toward a concept of the unitary nature of matter.

So, as religion shucks off prescientific speculations that have rigidified into dogma, it gets closer to seizing upon the concept of a universal spiritual reality which is as universal as the scientist's.

Nowadays no one expects that the United States will have a set of scientific principles different from, say, Germany or Japan. And although Communist countries have on occasion tried to meddle with their scientists, they have not by a jot or tittle altered the universality of scientific method or principle.

Yet in religion we often cling to the illusion that we—Christians or Jews or Muslims or Buddhists—have the one correct set of principles. Ours is the true science; the rest are superstitions or heresies. We have not yet reached the point of recognizing a universal truth above our particular dogmas. We still want the earth to stand still and the sun to move.

Yet if God is to be meaningful, he must be universal. He must be the goal of Christian and Muslim and Jew and Buddhist alike; otherwise our concept of God is too small to be godlike. And if this is so, then the pretense that one religion only can be true becomes a denial of God himself, and a sign of provincialism in those who so pretend.

There is a religion above religions which is in all religions. It recognizes the oneness of life both human and divine. It recognizes a unity of spirit as certain as the unity in matter. It welcomes spiritual insight from all sources. It recognizes that human preferences and human history have created and will continue to create many forms of religious expression, but that all yearn toward truth as plants turn to the sun. Meditation, because it is free of dogma, of historical commitments and narrow prejudices, because it is practised for the most part silently and therefore secretly, and because it is practised by some members of all religions—meditation is a channel for seekers of all faiths or no faith, a river into which many streams can freely flow, and from which the pure water of understanding can be drawn.

Well, then, what has meditation to do with the problem of the one and the many?

Since this is a problem which bedevils almost every area of

life, meditation will help to clarify, and to that extent to moderate or neutralize the difficulty. One might profitably meditate on one or all of these problems:

When five witnesses to an accident give contrary evidence, to what extent is their evidence true? Is there one truth? Are their perceptions true even when they conflict? Is there a subjective as well as an objective truth? Are both really true?

You hear a symphony and are moved by it. Someone you respect finds it dull. How can both responses be correct, or can they?

The maples on my lawn, all responding to the same influences and the same laws, put out their leaves at different times, even several weeks apart. How can they be so free with the necessity of their natures? Is there a parable here of personal differences? Of differences between religions?

Men have seen God in a burning bush, a sacred grove, an animal, as the spirit of earth or grain or river, in the heavens, in storm and in silence. Are all visions of God true, including animism, snake worship, human sacrifice? Where do we draw the line? How do we *know?*

Am I, in my beliefs, preserving my individuality or am I surrendering to the pressures of a society that is bent upon making me conform? How much must I insist upon for integrity? When I stand apart, am I just a crank or am I being true to something deep?

I sometimes feel a spiritual presence within myself. I sometimes feel it in nature. But how do I know they have anything to do with each other, or with God?

Said Umpati, a Hindu sage: "The soul is not merged in the Supreme, for if they become one, both disappear; if they remain two there is no fruition; therefore there is union and non-union."

Scientists also have a word for a similar situation, where some of the observed phenomena can be accounted for only by one theory, some by another—for example, the behavior of light.

They call this complementarity.

"Therefore there is union and non-union." Minds tuned to the full reality would no doubt find nothing puzzling in this, but our little minds, trained to the practice of either-or, black or white, good or bad, high or low, function by habit in great realms as in small, attempting to measure infinity with a yardstick.

Once during meditation I saw a patch of sky as if I had been at the bottom of a well looking up. Because it was spring, I saw daffodils as a fringe all around the well, but they were apparently there for beauty, not for any other use. Or were they there to complete the trinity? Man in the well, nature at the rim, God in the infinite beyond.

Why had I seen that tiny portion of blue sky? The only reason I know is that I was to learn from this the nature of the truth we see. Our human perceptions are limited, like the view you get of the sky from the bottom of a well. Yet the whole sky is there, waiting to be read. We can try to imagine what the rest of the sky must be like, but we shall never know. Or we can try to get out of the well.

One way is to meditate. Perhaps that is why the daffodils were there, encouraging me to try.

4

THINKING IN SYMBOLS

IN the cold of the year, a curious thing begins to happen to us. We are transformed by warmth, love, expectation, joy.

The days may be dark and gloomy, yet an air of anticipation and gladness takes charge of our hearts. Bells ring on street corners and in our breasts. We think of friends and relatives far distant, and send messages to them, and the message is one of joy. We scurry around during our lunch hour, looking into shops we hardly enter otherwise and consulting lists of names and notions. The stack of gifts accumulates in closets, bottom drawers, attics. Mystery sweeps into the house with the cold wind when a family member comes home; loving jokes are made over the clumsy, unhidable but secret bundles. We grow generous, even careless with our money. We grow kind and more forgiving, more forbearing.

What sort of miracle is this?

It is a demonstration of the power of a symbol.

The central symbol is an infant—an infant whose birth we foreknow by a magic we accept as matter-of-factly as the water which comes when we turn on the faucet. He will be born on the twenty-fifth of December. No—he was born on such a day, nearly two thousand years ago. Yet he will be born again—this year, as in every year since his first birth.

Churches throughout the world prepare for the event, with practice of special music and ritual, with decorations of green boughs and trees and a doll-infant surrounded by other figures of the story.

But the real center of the event is in the home—in every Christian home. Children, in anticipation, miraculously grow well-behaved. Small fingers essay large results with needle or hammer or paste. When the young are bedded, parents are drawn close together as they survey and wrap the surprises that will galvanize the young on Christmas morning. And on the eve of the great day, the tree is brought in, set up, decorated, surrounded with gifts. Each family has its own ritual for this—a ritual in part inherited, in part improvised to meet family needs, but regarded as sacred.

The lighting of the decorated tree will be one high moment, the placing of the gifts another, the gathering of the clan and opening of gifts another. Somewhere music, and perhaps prayer or recitations, will have a place. And at some time during the days of celebration the Christmas story will be heard. The guiding star, the stable, the birth, the baby, the shepherds, and the wise men with their gifts will merge miraculously with the tree, the lights, the gifts, the children of the gathered family. Somehow the family at Bethlehem becomes one with every rejoicing family.

No one notices how illogical it is to pretend that the infant, dead these two thousand years, has just been born. Or that the star, the shepherds, the wise men are performing all over again as if for the first time, their counterparts busy in every Christmas pageant. No one asks why the remnants of pagan celebrations, in the form of tree and yule log, have been allowed to intrude into this Christian affair. No one is bothered by the happy confusion which places the star in the east upon the top of a very pagan tree, or associates the lights on that tree with the light of the Gospel.

No one notices or minds because the magic of symbol is at work. It has transformed our hearts as old Scrooge was transformed. It has put love in the place of worry and fear. It has persuaded us, at least for the moment, that peace has come to men of good will. The light shines not only over Bethlehem, on all the trees, in windows and churches, but in our hearts.

Nor is this only a Christian festival. The Hindus have Diwali, the Jews their Feast of Lights, the Zoroastrians their eternal sacred fire, the Buddhists their lamps and lanterns, the Japanese their Obon. The festival of the return of light, often held at the dark of the year, is well-nigh universal.

The remarkable thing about this complex of symbols and our response to them is that they are as real to us as our own hands. They tie us to a world that is eternal and unchanging—that is always there, though we return to it but once a year. They anchor us to the grand cycle of the year and of the centuries, to events of cosmic grandeur and significance, to creation and the Creator, through one birth to every birth, through one child to all children, through one light to all light.

If a symbol or a set of symbols can do all this to us, it is clear that an understanding and use of symbols must be important to the art of meditation.

The story of Jesus' birth is a drama of light—"The true Light, which lighteth every man that cometh into the world," as John forewarns us.

And Zacharias, his mouth opened upon the birth of another John, his son, prophesies in images of light: "The dayspring from on high hath visited us, to give light to them that sit in darkness and in the shadow of death." (Luke 1:78, 79.)

This much is prologue. Then comes the birth, and then the angel's visit to the shepherds. "And the glory of the Lord shone round about them." After that, the star in the east, guiding the wise men. "And, lo, the star, which they saw in the east, went before them, till it came and stood over where the young child was." Then after the purification of Mary, Jesus was taken into the temple where Simeon, illumined by the holy spirit, saw in the baby "a light to lighten the Gentiles, and the glory of thy people Israel." (Luke 2:32.)

No one born to the Christian heritage and possessed of his birthright can fail to be moved by this feast of light, nor fail to connect it with Paul's "For God . . . hath shined in our hearts." Light is the imperial symbol for the divine, the Creator, whose sun is light, whose light permeates space to warm and lighten us. Its mysterious power of leaping through cold space to make contact with man and stir his senses is itself a wondrous symbol of a power that both transcends and dwells in man.

Much of the Bible is bathed in light. "God is light, and in him is no darkness at all. . . . If we walk in the light, as he is in the light, we have fellowship one with another." (I John 1:5, 7.) "Ye were sometimes darkness, but now are ye light in the Lord: walk as children of light." (Ephesians 5:8.) "I am the light of the world: he that followeth me shall not walk in darkness, but shall have the light of life." (John 8:12.)

The Psalms are full of light:

"Lord, lift thou up the light of thy countenance upon us." (4:6.)

"The Lord is my light and my salvation; whom shall I fear?" (27:1.)

"Thy word is a lamp unto my feet, and a light unto my path." (119:105.)

Strangely enough, the book of Job, which deals with the darkness of tragedy, has more references to light than any other single book. "Upon whom doth not his light arise?" (25:3.) "He will deliver his soul from going into the pit, and his life shall see the light." (33:28.) "Where is the way where light dwelleth? and as for darkness, where is the place thereof?" (38:19.)

So light becomes a symbol not only for godliness, but for the power of creation, for intelligence, salvation, divine guidance, conversion, life itself.

61

SYMBOLIC THINKING

But what has all this to do with meditation?

Meditation, for the most part, deals with words. And words are symbols. It is a powerful aid to meditation, therefore, to understand why words—often very plain ones—are full of power.

The moment I say, "the cross," a picture springs into your mind. It may be purely geometrical. Or it may be the cross on an altar, or over the door or on the steeple of a church, or it may be the cross in one of the great *quattrocento* paintings of Jesus at Golgotha. In any case this simple geometric figure of crossed lines will arouse thoughts of a man brutally nailed to a cross of wood, left there to suffer and to die, but in the course of his suffering speaking the words we still know, many of us by heart, after all these years. Yet it is a symbol to us, not only of suffering, but paradoxically of victory. "In the cross of Christ I glory, Towering o'er the wreck of time," says the old hymn. The instrument of an ignoble death has become the symbol of victory over death and of God's caring for man. How illogical! How is it that a symbol can accomplish so much?

In the early church the fish was an equally potent symbol. It, too, was easily drawn: . Christians meeting secretly could make contact by completing such a figure with stick or finger on the ground. But why a fish?

Jesus was, first of all, the God revealed in the water through baptism. He was the fisher of men, the companion of fishermen. His greatest miracles were associated with fish—feeding the multitudes, bringing in full nets where no fish had been caught. These miracles themselves suggest his connection with a cult of fertility.

More than this, the early church associated him with Jonah whom the whale had swallowed and then given up, thus providing a symbol of resurrection. The fish was also eaten in the sacred mystery and was to be eaten in the kingdom of God. So the fish stood for everything important in the faith—baptism, resurrection, eucharist, the kingdom to come, the miraculous powers, the Lord's providing for his elect.

Another early Christian symbol, now little known, was that of a lamb carrying a milk pail. The lamb, an animal of sacrifice, stood for the sacrifice and resurrection of Jesus. Milk symbolizes new birth and sacred food, and is associated with the milk and honey of the promised land. The convert to Christianity, through the communion ritual, is fed by the church. So all these meanings —sacrifice, new birth, resurrection and the heavenly kingdom —are brought together.

A symbol is a minor miracle in itself. It makes an intelligible whole of several aspects of reality. It unites people by giving them something that seems tangible, a sort of standard to rally to. It opens up levels of meaning and significance of which we are otherwise unaware. It starts with a simple, material thing and then plunges into depths of intuition and surmise and bold assumption. It reaches beyond everyday logic with a strange authority and graphic quality like that of a dream. It unites a childlike figure or concept with meanings that go out beyond our depth. It combines sensuous, emotional, intuitive and logical insights all together. It therefore demands total response.

Thought itself is indeed a symbolic process—a process of turning experience into words, ideas, pictures, abstractions, norms. To recognize as a chair everything going under that name requires quite a feat of symbol-making. "Symbolization," says Susanne Langer, "is the essential act of mind." [1] She goes on to point out that every mind is furnished with an enormous store of symbolic materials which may be used in various ways or not at all, existing simply as a result of spontaneous brain activity and forming a reserve fund of conceptions. It is from this reservoir of mental wealth that meditation, indeed, draws.

[1] *Philosophy in a New Key,* Mentor Book, 1948, p. 33.

And as we practise meditation we learn to draw on it more and more. Yet the reservoir never goes dry. Symbolic thought appears very early in human culture. Tabu, myth, fairy tale, patterns on pottery and basketry, rites and scapegoats, and indeed language itself—all are symbolic.

A symbol does not *mean* the object it refers to. It means much more than that. A symbol is the instrument by which we conceive an object and give it meaning. We may thus symbolize two crossed lines as the plus sign or the multiplying sign in arithmetic, as a wooden structure, as an instrument of torture, or as the sign of Christ's victory over death. All are true. The more symbolic meanings cluster about an object, the richer its meaning for us.

Why then do we have symbols? We have them first of all because thought itself requires them, is formed by them. Mental process requires simple forms it can store and codify, as an IBM machine transforms information to holes in a card. But on a deeper level we have symbols because we seek security and reassurance in a world which is in many ways hostile. We need a picture of life which gives meaning to the world of nature and man, and which promises us some kind of security in it. We need a way of relating ourselves to the stars, the past, the seasons, nature, mankind, and the future, which is meaningful. In our own time, with its uprootedness, urbanization, and separation from the earth and the means of providing our own food or living in a family home hallowed by generations, most of us are in greater need than ever of finding symbols which will make life significant.

"Religion," says Durkheim, "is, first and foremost, a system of ideas by means of which individuals can envisage the society of which they are members, and the relations, obscure yet intimate, which they bear to it. That is the primordial task of a faith. And though it be metaphorical and symbolical, it is not therefore untrue. On the contrary, it conveys all that is essen-

64

tial in the relations it claims to portray." [2] As the making of symbols is essential to human thought, so the making of religious symbols is in this view essential to the functioning of the individual in society.

Symbolism was once regarded as a form of religious thinking. Now religion is regarded by many scholars as a form of symbolic thinking. If this disturbs the orthodox, it may be set aside, but it opens up a new path to those who have felt strangled by orthodoxy; it frees them to search all religion and all religions for symbols that may be significant in their own search for certainty.

All religious language is symbolic. Religion lives by its symbols and can communicate in no other way. The danger is that, while symbols are intended to point beyond to the deeper reality and to make us feel it, we may content ourselves with the symbol and fail to leap beyond it. So we stop with the cross on the altar, the image in the niche, the established church.

Symbols are results of a creative encounter with reality, as Paul Tillich points out, and God is the symbol of our encounter with the ground of our being, with ultimate reality.

In *The Meaning of History* Nicholas Berdyaev shows that the knowledge of the divine life cannot be reached by logic and abstract thought, but only by way of a concrete myth which sees the divine life as "a passionate destiny of concrete and active persons."

"Only a mythology, which conceives the divine celestial life as celestial history and as a drama of love and freedom unfolding itself between God and His other self, which He loves and for whose reciprocal love He thirsts, and only an admission of God's longing for His other self, can provide a solution of celestial history, and, through it, of the destinies of both man and the world." (P. 52.)

[2] Quoted in Susanne Langer, *op. cit.* p. 134.

Meditation: The Inward Art

The triumph of Christianity over previous religions lay in its ability to achieve this, exalting man above the elemental nature with which previous religions of creativeness and fertility had been concerned.

But humanism, by regarding man again as part of nature, divorced him from the divine center of his life. It thus constituted an attack upon man as well as God. "For man ceases to know himself when he knows of no higher being or other principles than those contained in the confined circle of his nature." (P. 155.) "To create beauty in this world we must situate the real center of mankind in another world. The most beautiful creations of mankind have been determined, not by purely terrestrial aims and relations, but by a purpose set up beyond the limits of the natural world." (P. 201.)

The trouble is that every human culture shows a tendency to disintegrate its religious and spiritual foundations, to repudiate its own symbolism. And that is the trouble we are in now. That is why, more than ever, we need personal meditation to connect us directly with the deep certainties that lie submerged below consciousness. The certainties are there as surely as they were in Plato's time, or Buddha's, or Saint Augustine's. But with the eroding of the public symbols of religion, we have to make the private search ourselves. We cannot, as in moments of great religious fervor, be borne along with the crowd.

The fact that we can now more easily know all the world religions and the variety of symbols by which they try to lead their believers to God may be upsetting to those who feel that the religion they were raised in must be true and others spurious, or that if there can be so many religions, perhaps none is true. But this is to mistake the importance of symbol. Each culture must make its own as each man, ultimately, must. The variety of symbols is a testimony to the great variety and creativity of the divine gift in man. Though God is one, and the idea of Him binds all believers, He is also "this, and this, and this." Each believer cherishes his own, but even in the sum of these, God is not reached. For by definition God must be beyond all limiting definitions.

The truly religious person, mindful of all the facts of history that lead to variety, honors religious insight and faith in all its forms. For somewhere within and yet beyond all this faith, all this reaching for God, the divine exists. Every path leads to the mountain, but there is more to the mountain than is comprised in all the paths. Yet he who knows all the paths, best knows the mountain.

By a study of all the symbols that have been associated with religion—the cross, the fish, the lotus, the torii, the Parthenon, the cathedral, the lingam, the broken bread, the offerings of food and incense—we come gradually to see that similar impulses and insights have been at work, however various the results. In our own time, Gandhi has been the supreme maker of symbols. The *charkha* (spinning wheel) and daily spinning awoke a whole nation to the idea that they could help themselves, use their idle time, and resist the influence of the imperial ruler and his economic dominance. Gandhi's march to the sea to make salt against the British laws and salt tax was a magnificent assertion of man's natural rights. So in America the sit-in has provided a dignified and nonviolent symbol of the right of a minority to equal treatment—a symbol of action morally undertaken to defend the truth that all men are equal under God.

Such symbols may not be, strictly speaking, religious, but they illustrate the way symbols can assert moral positions.

While I was living in India I had the privilege of joining a Hindu family at their morning prayers. When we entered the room, the grandmother had already begun the ceremony, feeding a little fire with sticks, throwing in bits of food and spice, and chanting by memory from one of the holy books. Then her son, taking his place across the fire, picked up the chant. For more than half an hour they carried it on from memory, still feeding the fire. I could not tell what they were saying, but I felt a religious presence—a familiar, friendly, almost offhand communication with God. The ghee poured upon the little fire does not mean as much to me as the broken bread and the wine taken in remembrance, but clearly their purpose is the same.

Not only the bread and wine, but the living water, the vine and its branches, the good seed, the lost farthing, the light hid under a bushel, the lost sheep, the multiplied loaves and fishes, the house built upon rock, the wise and foolish virgins, the talents, the strewn palms, the cross, the sepulchre, the pierced hands— all these symbols, rich with human meaning, so commonplace and yet so illuminated with the divine presence through the Teacher's application of them, have gripped men's hearts through the centuries. They have much to do with the impact and the spread of Christianity. Symbols which by their immediacy and closeness to everyday experience can be grasped by anyone, and which by their sudden expansion of meaning draw us up to the divine—these are the life blood of a vital religion.

WHAT SYMBOLS DO

Symbols, by making the commonplace sacramental—sharing food, serving our neighbor, bathing—domesticate the divine, bring it to the workaday level. Perhaps one of the best things religious symbolism can do is to show us how the everyday is divine, and how every activity partakes of it.

This, actually, is what happens with the most significant symbols in the end. We break bread, not only at the altar, but in our homes. Because of the Last Supper, every meal is memorial. And the Last Supper is significant because we must eat and be filled, not only with the daily bread but with the bread of righteousness and truth. Symbol elevates daily life to the spiritual plane. The cross is not only a symbol, but the reminder of an historic fact. The sufferer on the cross was no symbol; he was a living man. His suffering, however, symbolizes the suffering of all humanity, the cruelty of man to man, the divine involvement in this mystery of suffering which the sacrifice of Jesus helps us to bear but does not explain. So symbol at its best begins at home, grapples with the mystery that is in all experience, and grasps for the sky.

Symbols can help make reality more real as a smile put on for company may help to induce a friendliness one does not at first truly feel. So the sacredness of food and the family meal is enhanced by the ritual Jesus made of the Last Supper. So in our meditations we can use the symbols that mean most to us—sunset, favorite prospect, falling water, music, the sculptured beauty of the human body, a child's laughter—as steppingstones to the divine.

Acts that are symbolic can shape events. Gandhi's symbolic daily spinning helped bring on India's independence. Socrates' refusal to escape jail and death dignifies every philosopher and encourages every testimony to truth on trial.

Symbols are not toys. They are the rocket charges that impel history. And life will be richer if we seek out the symbols that mean most to us and live by them. Everyone responds to the flag, to the picture of his Capitol or the Statue of Liberty. Similarly, symbols of the state and the town we live in help to bind us together as a people. But what symbol in the political sphere might help us to realize the universal brotherhood our religion tells us to accept?

A serious search for symbols of unity might prove the most fruitful form of meditation in a time where failure to achieve that unity literally threatens the extinction of mankind. But to do this, we must learn to see what is meant by the symbols of others, especially those we are farthest from in politics or religion.

The tragedy of organized religions is that they have pushed their own symbols as exclusive truth. For these particular symbols men have fought and killed each other. Yet a religious

war is a bitter contradiction: men slaying each other in the
name of a god each recognizes as universal—yet his own exclusive possession! How do we arrive at the revelation that God
is one, no matter how many names he is given? How do we learn
to accept universalism and still retain our own parochialism as
a matter of choice and birthright, being sympathetic to all religions and active in the search for symbols that will unite us all?
One answer: through meditation.

"All things are artificial, for nature is the art of God." For
me, this illuminates all of life. It expresses the essential symbolism of religion itself as a glass through which man looks at life
and sees it more clearly. Or one might regard all religion as the
symbol of man's noble, pathetic, grand, unending effort to understand, to find meaning in existence, to probe with his small talents
the great secrets of being. Yet it is this very effort which makes
him a little like God, which joins him to God. "In the beginning
was the Word"—that is, speech, ideas, concepts, understanding.

THE SYMBOLISM OF LOVE

The other thing that joins man to God is love. No religion of
consequence has failed to see this. "Thou shalt love the Lord
thy God." "God so loved the world." The teachings of Jesus
centered on emotional unity through love. He tried to create
an emotional culture in which all divisive thoughts and feelings
would be overcome by love. Moti's reciprocal love and the
Buddha's compassion come to mind as other examples. Where
the Jewish system had been based on an extension of family
unity to the tribes of Israel, Jesus taught that the covenant with
God could be extended by voluntary agreement to include all
men everywhere. Here was the beginning of the voluntarism and
democracy which has been the main current of human history
despite all the dictators and authoritarians.

Before Jesus, God was conceived and symbolized as father,

as patriarch. Jesus showed the importance of brotherly emotion in the working out of a common purpose.[3] It must have seemed absurd in his time to propose that men of different races should worship one God and be united like brothers. Yet all divisive feelings were (at least for a time) washed away in baptism and in breaking bread together as believers.

The first churches, as we see them through the eyes of Paul, had this sense of unity. The first apostles represent the truly democratic emotional culture.

"A new commandment I give unto you, That ye love one another; as I have loved you, that ye also love one another. By this shall all men know that ye are my disciples, if ye have love one to another." (John 13:34, 35.)

Jesus sought a way to make men feel so close to each other that when one was hurt, all felt the pain. If such an emotional culture could be created, men would rise to what is divine within them, and make government a matter not only of laws and protection, but of familial care. Here again symbols can help. "All men are brothers." The symbol of brotherhood, if only we could achieve as well as conceive it, would represent the goal of most religions.

Significant symbolism is rooted in the family and family relationships. To an infant, the mother's warm breast and responsive nipple, her encircling arms and her lap represent safety, food, life, love, and contact with the world outside. The female breast continues to arouse men, not only because its form is so beautifully suited to its function, but because the infant dependency has developed into an awareness of all the things symbolized.

Motherhood itself becomes symbolic of other relationships as the infant grows into childhood. Nurturing the growing child, teachers become extensions of the mother, and the school itself is symbolized as alma mater, tender mother.

[3] See J. H. Denison's *Emotion as the Basis of Civilization,* New York, 1928, a tremendously helpful book.

Meditation: The Inward Art

From the family arise the other significant relations—father to son, mother to daughter, brother to brother, older sister to younger brother. Upon them man has built his societies—some patriarchal, others matriarchal. The idea of the state as a father or mother to a whole tribe or race is illustrated wherever we look. In ancient Israel, God was the stern father who gave the laws and punished the offender. In a monarchy the king usually claimed some sort of divine sanction or descent. And even Shakespeare gave frequent testimony to the divinity that doth hedge a king.

We speak of the father of our country, of the town fathers. So family relationships make political organization understandable and emotionally acceptable. In religion, too, it is the emotionally entrenched family relationships which give intensity and significance to God the father, Jesus his son, and Mary the mother of Jesus. Our most important human relationships become the symbolic foundation for our politics and our religion.

Years ago I attended the Orthodox service of a Russian congregation in New York. During the communion service the priest, a benevolent and fatherly looking man dressed in splendid brocaded robes, received a baby into his arms. Attendants brought a gold-brocaded bib. The priest, taking a golden baby's spoon, dipped some of the communion wine from the cup and spooned a few drops into the baby's mouth. I learned later that this was regarded as a cure for some infant ailment. But it was a charming symbolic act. The priest, acting as the deputy of God the father, in transmitting the sacred liquid would bring God's healing grace to this infant body. Something of this healing power is in every communion and in every shared meal where grace is said.

The sharing of any meal is a family symbol of interdependence and love, and there is hardly a religion that does not use food in some holy, symbolic way.

Ancient rites make clear the compulsion to build symbols

that will explain and even affect the mystery of life, fertility, sexual union. It is almost as if men had no other way to grapple with the great mysteries. Indeed, the power to symbolize is the root of all poetry, art, science and mathematics. For mathematics is nothing but a symbol system. And what are the protons, neutrons and positrons of modern physics, or the formulae of Einstein? In symbol, moreover, we confront the mysterious core of mental process—a process by which man unites himself to the universe in a way that is little short of miracle. The poet, the prophet, the musician, the scientist, and the ancient husbandman are bound together by their use of symbol.

5

PARABLES AS MEDITATION

ONE form of meditation everybody knows: the parable. Even Biblical illiterates, and they are now many, know by hearsay at least of the good Samaritan, the prodigal son, the lost sheep, the ten pieces of silver, the talents, the wise and foolish virgins.

Although Jesus used the parable as a teaching device, there is no reason why it cannot serve as a gateway to meditation in two ways.

First, we read the parable meditatively. Let us read that of the good Samaritan, so brief, so beautiful, so rich in meanings.

"A certain man went down from Jerusalem to Jericho, and fell among thieves, which stripped him of his raiment, and wounded him, and departed, leaving him half dead. And by chance there came down a certain priest that way: and when he saw him, he passed by on the other side. And likewise a Levite, when he was at the place, came and looked on him, and passed by on the other side.

"But a certain Samaritan, as he journeyed, came where he was: and when he saw him, he had compassion on him, and went to him, and bound up his wounds, pouring in oil and wine, and set him on his own beast, and brought him to an inn, and took care of him. And on the morrow when he departed, he took out two pence, and gave them to the host, and said unto him, 'Take care of him; and whatsoever thou spendest more, when I come again, I will repay thee.' " (Luke 10:30–35.)

Well, everyone immediately gets the story itself and the moral implication. Erring Christians that we are, we have all been influenced by this story to be a little better than we would otherwise be. But there is much else in it.

Everyone knows, of course, that "Samaritan" was a laughing word in the days of Jesus, as if we should say, in older phrase, a hayseed, or now perhaps a square. So virtue may appear where we least expect it.

But by what right do we call people squares or Samaritans? Are we better than they? To what extent do I appear as a Samaritan to others, either in the good or the bad sense? Since the word Samaritan, once used in disrespect, has come to mean for us a compassionate man, can we by our behavior change the meaning of Kike or Canuck or Dago by refusing to play a part in the conspiracy of prejudice? Or is it not open to us to change the meaning of our own names, now and at any time, simply by being more than we have hitherto been?

The moral about those who pass by on the other side is obvious enough. But how about the other ways we pass by on the other side? The beauty we close our eyes to? The moment when we might have stopped for a friendly exchange instead of rushing to the next encounter, the next appointment? The way we let the childhood of our young ones slip irrevocably by without taking the time to participate in it? The elders we never visit until it is too late? The time we should have set aside for peace, for joy, for meditation?

"When he saw him, he had compassion on him." Let us again reach beyond the obvious moral. All these things the Samaritan does come of his sense of the oneness of life and the privilege of sharing it. There is more than one way of being wounded, more than one way of binding up the wounds of misfortune, disadvantage, discrimination.

"When I come again, I will repay thee." But how often do we try to get off without giving of our best, or congratulate ourselves when we get the best of the other fellow?

All these are obvious points for meditation. But the whole parable moves to another level if we think of the relationship between the human and the divine. Then the good Samaritan, like the good shepherd, is the fathering spirit who stoops down, who binds up, lodges and cares for all. Or who, at life's end, takes the individual who has been laid low by the blows of life —takes him to himself. Or again, the whole story might be seen as a spiritual journey with its hazards and its ultimate rewards.

These are only hints. One might take a single phrase, such as "Take care of him," and build a whole meditation upon it. What does it mean to take care of a person? Who cares for whom? Is it more blessed to give than to receive? Why? How many things we mean by care!

"Martha, Martha, thou art careful and troubled about many things." (Luke 10:41.) That kind of care.

Or the person who is full of cares.

Or the kind expressed by "Do you really care for me?"

Still different if expressed, "Do you really care about me?"

Who cares?

She cares for her mother.

Have a care!

All from that beautiful word, *caritas,* love.

THINKING BY PARABLE

Parable is a rewarding form of thought. It is deceptively simple. The story it tells is immediately understood and direct in its impact. Yet its deeper meanings continue to vibrate and to disclose themselves long after—perhaps throughout life. Narrative is a direct form of communication, imitating the experience it presents. Analysis, criticism, and moral may be implicit, but they are organic to the story.

If, therefore, we could develop the art of thinking in parables

76

as Jesus did, we would have a powerful instrument of meditation in our hands.

Let us try.

A certain man had two children, of whom the elder was a boy, the younger a girl. And the father died, so that the children were parted to distant places. And as the girl grew to womanhood it was seen that she was fair. And her fairness was as a lure, that men might vie with each other to see which should have her. And her head was turned, and her vanity puffed up, and by flattery she was drawn into a wood and seduced. And others, when they heard of her fall, vied the more until they in like wise had flattered and seduced her.

And her brother, going to a far city, learned by the devices of flattery and emulation to succeed in the city's ways, until he was rich and powerful, and anything that he asked was his.

Hearing then of a famous courtesan who had but recently come to that city, he visited her that he might have knowledge of her, and if she pleased him, add her to his great possessions.

And he came in to her and found her fair and knew her. And he took her to his home and gave her rich apartments and many servants, and his heart was smitten almost beyond enduring, for he found in her some echo of himself, and it was as a mystery to him.

But on an evening when they lay in each other's arms, speaking of the past, it grew upon them that they were brother and sister. And yet he could not bear to part from her, for now the secret of that oneness was clear to him, and they had been too long parted.

"Did not the Egyptians marry brother and sister together?" he said. "And shall we fear to do as they did?"

And he caused a great wedding to be prepared, and married her, and raised her out of her degradation, and got children upon her, and placed them well, and died in his time, full of years.

77

Meditation: The Inward Art

This all came as a surprise to me, from what source or reason I know not. Its end was somehow implicit in its beginning, which came quite spontaneously just as I have set it down here. If I were trying to be edifying, perhaps I would destroy it and substitute something else. But I am trying to open a way to deeper meditation, and I must be honest.

It is true that I thought first of writing, "A certain man had two sons." But that thought was rejected before it was set down. Once the boy and girl came into being, the rest followed without effort. As it went on, I thought I saw in it a parable of seduction. The girl, seduced by flattery, would lose her reputation. The boy, becoming a rich businessman, would in the world's esteem gain a high reputation. They would meet. He would reproach her with having fallen, and she in turn would point out that the tricks he had used to gain his high place were no better than hers; that both had prostituted themselves to things of the flesh and had missed the way.

That would have made a good parable. But it didn't turn out that way. An undercurrent of revolt set in which brought the two to peaks of success in their lines and then to the sin of incest, regarded with the utmost horror in our civilization, though not in several others besides the ancient Egyptian; the Hawaiians, for example, also regarded brother-sister marriages as the highest kind of union. So out of this horror came family solidarity and a good end.

Hidden in this parable is a sense of the inevitable twinning of life—of male and female, brother and sister, vanity and flattery, loved and lover, brother and lover, father and husband, good and evil. There is the idea that the spirit seeks its own, and knows its own beyond any disguising. There is the curious manner in which the brother saves the girl from prostitution and raises her to wifehood, with its suggestion of generosity and compassion even though the motive seems to be passion. There is the aura of corruption which overcomes and seems near to sinking the young innocents, who, however, triumph by mastering the arts of corruption without, apparently, ever quite becoming sunk in them. And then, out of all this corruption—even of incest (and must it not be true that human life began in incest? Whom did Adam's sons marry?)—a sound family arises.

Out of evil good can come, even out of the evil we think beyond the pale. No man, no woman is beyond redemption, for love is redeeming.

It is, perhaps, a strange story to propagate these truths. Yet its strangeness may be what makes them stand out.

To let a series of such parables well up out of the subconscious and then to seek their inner meaning could be a revelatory kind of meditation. Similarly dreams, which also embody subconscious meanings in story or parable form, could provide rich fields for meditation if fearlessly confronted.

6

MEDITATION AND THE ARTS

THE ideal of the artist is beauty
—at least it used to be before painters began dribbling paint
and walking in it, or composers making noises on tape. The ideal
of the scientist is truth, and of the moralist, goodness. Any one
of these ideals is worth the devotion of a lifetime, yet no one
of them alone can satisfy man's thirst for wholeness. In Hindu
thought, these three comprise the qualities of the soul. If they
are indeed within us, then the work of the artist, the scientist,
and the moralist or social reformer is a response to an inner
urge and an inner vision that must be in some degree present before he takes up his career.

The total vision, which comprises all three—beauty, truth and
the good—is what we call religion. The wholeness from which
such a vision proceeds, we call God. If moderns could only accept that, and stop worrying the idea of God as if they had to
shake the life out of it, they could get on with being. True worship lies in recognizing the holiness of wholeness. True meditation lies in the effort to grasp that vision.

It is likely that the word "religion" is based upon the same
root that gives us ligament and ligature. So it means to tie, to
bind. Dictionaries usually derive the word from re-, meaning
back, and lig-, meaning to bind. But re- also means anew. "To
bind anew." Isn't this what religion really tries to do?—to bind
truth and beauty and goodness together in one vision, to make

80

us aware of wholeness, and thus to make us whole? And to do all this in such a way as to renew our bonds of union with the true, the good, the beautiful?

Great works of art, of science, or of ethics, are invariably simple in design. Einstein's $E = mc^2$ may be beyond our comprehension if we are not physicists, but at least we can see the beauty in a vision which, after a great deal of hard work aided by imagination of a high order, has reduced a whole universe of phenomena to this brief formula. A Bach fugue may be wonderfully complex, but there is no senseless ornamentation, no superfluity. The Ten Commandments have a rocklike integrity and simplicity. Works which depend upon elaboration and ornamentation are, almost by definition, of second rank.

"Simplify, simplify!" This is the word the inner voice whispers to any creative worker—to Darwin, dealing with thousands of apparently irrelevant facts, to Einstein, to Phidias, to Plato, to Spinoza, to Buddha, to those Chinese and Japanese artists who excelled in the art of suggestion, to the builders of our functional modern buildings, to the unknown authors of folk ballads, the makers of machinery and every sort of device, down to the cap on a bottle or a child's toy. What mechanical toy wonder has ever surpassed a ball?

Whatever is truly great is truly simple. But the path to simplicity may be a long path, and a cluttered one. Before current atomic theory, we had the atomism of Democritus and Lucretius. Before the discovery of microorganisms, all kinds of elaborate ideas about the causes of illness.

Meditation ought to help steer us back onto the path of simplicity, ought to help us to distinguish between the necessary and the meretricious, the functional and the purely ornamental. "Simplify, simplify!" We ought to hear this reminder ringing in our heads as we consider what is needful for us to do, to achieve, to think about, to admire. Meditation, itself an art, will help us to live artistically. This means cutting out what is harmful or useless, and living far more intensely, every moment, on a higher plane. But how?

"Beauty is only skin-deep." This half truth is obviously man's effort to denigrate woman at her most sensitive point. But the beauty we all seek is as deep as God. The search for significance, for simplicity is an esthetic search. In seeking to live lives that are well ordered, uncluttered, harmonious, planned, we are seeking to fulfill an ideal of beauty that is somehow already within us.

How did it come there? Why do we respond to good order and harmoniousness?

Perhaps because we see them in nature—in the round of the seasons, in the motions of sun and stars, in the repetitions of heart beat and breath and birdsong, in the symmetry of bodies and trees and snowflakes. Primitive art tends to emphasize symmetry and regularity—a sure sign of the respect that is felt for them. So does primitive folksong with its repetition of words and phrases.

Poetry, too, has its pulse. In this brief poem of Robert Frost,[1] we can easily feel the heart beat, the simplicity, the concern for beauty.

> *Nature's first green is gold,*
> *Her hardest hue to hold.*
> *Her early leaf's a flower;*
> *But only so an hour.*
> *Then leaf subsides to leaf.*
> *So Eden sank to grief,*
> *So dawn goes down to day.*
> *Nothing gold can stay.*

It is so simply done, anyone might have done it—so it seems. Obvious in rhyme, in metre, in diction, it is yet so true in its

[1] From *Complete Poems of Robert Frost.* Copyright 1923 by Holt, Rinehart and Winston, Inc. Copyright renewed 1951 by Robert Frost. Reprinted by permission of Holt, Rinehart and Winston, Inc.

observation and in its unexpected moral dimension that one suddenly finds the three things merged: truth, beauty, the good.

This unforgettable little poem is also a perfect gem of meditation. You begin with something that strikes upon your attention—the special beauty of the gold-green leaf of early spring. Why, it puts out a sort of flower before the true leaf forms! The first leaf passes, impermanent as Eden to Adam. The poet's world has suddenly enlarged now, throwing him back to mankind's dawn. And then to the day's dawn, also impermanent and passing. Then suddenly the last line draws it all together in an assertion which is simple and deep, as true of man's ambitions as of the shifting face of nature.

From the specific we have been led by skillful stages to the universal. This is what meditation should do.

The following brief poem of Emily Dickinson has a similar effect.

> *Each that we lose takes part of us;*
> *A crescent still abides,*
> *Which like the moon, some turbid night,*
> *Is summoned by the tides.*

The method of the poet is good training for the meditator. Although we may lack the skills of the poet, we can cultivate his sensitivity to man and nature, and keep our eyes open for those little things out of which poems are made—the new leaves, the bent birches, the roads diverging in a wood, the leaves in a spring, the stones tumbled off a wall. Robert Frost used materials available to anyone who has ever walked in the country.

While I was meditating one day, I remembered the boyhood thrill of tree climbing. Suddenly the meaning of it came clear, and without much effort the memory worked itself out in a poem. It would be a better poem if it were shorter, I suspect, but I am willing to expose it here to give a working example of a by-product of meditation.

Meditation: The Inward Art

CLIMBING TREE

In every youthtime there must be,
Just as in mine, a climbing tree.

Not every tree will do for climbing.
The elm's no good—it goes too swiftly up
Without the friendly notch to cup
A groping foot, a grappling hand.
Birch bends, and coltlike sets you back on land,
While oak's too kingly proud to raise a ladder
Toward heaven to make a mere boy gladder.

Apple is good to learn on. Like a mother
It's there at need to brace each foot, one after other:
A good tree to browse in, best in appletime,
A tree for sidewise motion to the tip,
Then when the branch begins to dip,
Squatting and grasping where one stood,
Swinging above the earth, if in the mood,
Then dropping so hard the shock goes up from sole to eye
And stings like tears though lids stay dry.

Matriculate of apple,
I came at last, one wonder-morn, to grapple
In a clean grove, in shine of sun and leaf shadow,
With a tree though twenty times my height
That seemed my size and shape, and right.
Maple, with branches that went both out and up,
Full of sharp stirrups where sneakered feet could lodge,
Free of impertinent foliage to dodge,
Clean at the trunk, full-leafed in a green shroud.

Shroud-hidden, stretching my length from limb to limb,
Then hugging the trunk in ecstasy of height,
I climbed into a tree world of delight
Where branch and bone grew one and light was half night,
Where limb grew fast to limb and trunk to trunk

While blood and sap together coursed aloud
And leaves sucked up my carboned breath
And what I climbed on was both life and death.

Then, bruised and breathing as if from too much love,
Muscles atwitch and tree asway, above
I saw the green shroud fall away.
Hot from the climb, cold from the triumph that is fear,
And from finding the sky so near,
I dared at last look on the squashed world below—
Roofs jammed down on houses, flowers in a flattened row.

I felt my roots in earth, my leaves against the sky;
I sucked the damp earth like a babe at breast,
I pumped the sweet sap to each leafy crest.
I drank the sunlight in a green summer's dream;
My leafed lips whispered to the whispering stream.
For he who climbs becomes the tree—
How could it hold him else, or how could he
Hold all of it, both root and trunk and sky?

Rubric of love, that loosens what it binds,
Forever wedding clinging limbs to soaring minds.

The poem discovered, like a meditation, the identity of the boy with the tree, the sense of oneness with nature that comes to children perhaps with greater force than to adults; and beyond that, the nature of love itself. Some day I must try to make it shorter!

The poem comes close to expressing the interpenetration of God and man through the symbols of the boy and the tree, but perhaps doesn't quite succeed in conveying it. Yet in the back of my mind, I believe, was a sense not only of the climber becoming the tree, and of man clinging to his source, but of the leaf that is uttered from the branch, in turn issuing from the trunk, in turn nurtured by earth, air and sun. So perhaps we, too, are uttered from the source, from the same ultimate source.

We may be reminded of John's "I am the true vine, and my Father is the husbandman. . . . As the branch cannot bear fruit of itself, except it abide in the vine; no more can ye, except ye abide in me. I am the vine, ye are the branches: He that abideth in me, and I in him, the same bringeth forth much fruit: for without me ye can do nothing." (15:1–5.)

The innate sense of the beautiful that is within us will respond, if we let it, to beauty in nature or art or childhood, to the symmetries of scientific law and the social structures man builds in order to climb toward his dream of the good.

The flowers in my garden take their symmetry, their complex yet unified structures, for granted. I cannot help seeing in them a triumph of design which combines utility with beauty, and a way of life which ties them not only to sun and soil and air but to all plant life, to the seasons, to the insects which in feeding upon them scatter their fertility and hence become their wings. Why their color? Why this particular, delightful shade of color? Does the bee or the hummingbird know cerulean blue from rose-purple? "Consider the lilies of the field," said Jesus, finding in their casual yet godly beauty a promise that man too will be clothed and fed. "Seek ye first the kingdom of God, and his righteousness; and all these things shall be added unto you." (Matthew 6:33.)

Watch the mists rise from a mountain valley in the early morning, opening the view ahead bit by bit, hiding part of a hill with a finger of cloud, settling into the pockets between the hills until the sun breaks through and drives them out. So doubts dissolve and perplexities disappear before the light of the intellect shining into the quiet mind.

A baby's fingers clutch and will not let you go. So small a fellow for so stout a grip! So stout, and yet so needy. As are we. Can we not grasp what we need with equal strength and faith? Why not?

ART, SYMBOL, MEDITATION

Art, of course, is a form of symbolic thinking in which the creator tries to render his experience and his vision of reality through symbols he hopes will be as full of meaning to others as to himself. The first leaves, the diverging paths, the tree for climbing, the lilies of the field—they must carry us to a higher level of significance than themselves or they have failed. A poem, a painting, a piece of music is a bait with which we hope to catch something larger, a hook with which we grapple for things that are deep and lost, though somehow we know they are there.

Art itself thus becomes a symbol of reality, linking the material and particular with the spiritual and general. As God's art is nature, so our nature is art: what we seize with symbols comes to life in the mind. The nature God has made with his art, we perceive with ours, and so complete the circle back to the idea, the word out of which creation came. With our art we imitate what God with his art creates. Our creation may be secondary, but it is none the less real. Since art is the link between the human and the divine, no wonder the early philosophers thought of the artist as God-inspired.

Because art is symbolic thinking, each art has its special vocabulary and speech. The drama is symbolic action; as it presents a particular man doing a particular thing, we know it speaks of all men and all similar human actions. Music, as Susanne Langer has put it, is "our myth of the inner life." It goes beyond words to catch the fluid, changing, wordless moods and feelings for which there is no other vocabulary. Unless it is the dance, which combines action with music, again to suggest moods and movements that are beyond words.

Painting works with another vocabulary—of colors and forms that, no matter how they suggest motion, are static, nevertheless opening up another chamber of the mind. Here abstract or natural forms make a whole world. Pleasure and meaning come from form itself abstracted from human presence or movement.

But what has all this to do with meditation?

Merely this, that meditation is itself an art, and the way one goes about making a poem, a picture, or a piece of music is not very different from meditating. Perhaps the only difference is that meditation, except in Quaker Meeting, is not likely to be brought forth where others can share it.

There are advantages to the secretness and aloneness of meditation. We can face things about ourselves we might not be willing to share with others, except in a disguised symbolic form —which is what many writers are doing when they convert disruptions of childhood or marital disaster into fiction. We sometimes catch intimations of our relatedness to the universe too tenuous to be put in words. We may be overcome with a wordless feeling of bliss or well-being.

But many meditations would be helpful to others if they could be shared. And a good meditation may ask to be written out.

KEEPING A JOURNAL

When your meditation is over and you feel like setting it down, write it as you recall it, even if in telegraphic style. Don't be alarmed if it looks considerably less impressive in writing than you had supposed. This is the discouragement all writers learn to live with. Keep up the habit for months, for years, if it gives you pleasure.

Written meditations have several advantages. You will feel, for one thing, that you are accomplishing something—that your meditation time has not been wasted. Seeing your thoughts in writing will expose fallacies or weaknesses, and therefore lead to a strengthening of your meditative muscle. One meditation will nourish another, as organic compost from last year strengthens this year's garden.

Continuing practice in writing out your meditations will make your thinking grow more precise and seizable. The writing itself will improve, and this will help you in whatever field you express yourself. Better self-expression will increase your confidence and sense of knowing who and what you are and what your goals are. And this will reflect back into each new meditation. You will note an improvement in wording, in precision, in the form the meditation takes. Instead of being, as at first, a rather formless ramble over a flat landscape, it will become a purposeful climb up the mountain of some mental, moral or personal problem to—or near—the summit of solution, or at least of clarification, which is a form of solution.

Most people burn themselves out worrying over crises that never materialize or avoiding problems that could be dissolved or at least improved if faced. One of the great benefits of meditation is that it teaches us to face problems, drawing upon the divine inwardness for help. Every meditation increases this inner strength.

MEDITATING ON WORKS OF ART

Meditation, moreover, is the ground out of which works of art grow. Not only poetry, as we have seen, but music—consider such supreme works of meditation as Bach's "O man, bewail thy grievous sin," of the balanced calm of the Aphrodite of Melos (Venus de Milo), or the great religious paintings of Michelangelo. However secular, or even crazy, a work of art may seem to be, the creator must have meditated its form, structure and intent, and then have sought the best way to body forth his idea. Works of art therefore make good objects for meditation. As the viewer or listener reaches back through the object to identify himself with the creator's intent, he is joining himself to that great chain of being in which a particular creator is but a link.

Studying works of art will not only provide ideas to meditate upon. It will also awaken us to a sense of form, of order, of dramatic contrasts and parallels, of the stimulus of colors, shapes, sounds, rhythms, tones, images, symbols. Be aware! Be aware! This is what meditation demands of us—a full use of those divine powers we take for granted, then blunt by disuse. It is the woodsman's ax that is always sharp—not that of the suburbanite who rarely takes his from the rack.

Perhaps you will feel the urge to write a poem, paint a picture, compose a tune. Good! You need not expect them to be masterpieces. They may not be publishable, but having uttered them will have been a good experience. Meditation will both help and be helped by them. The nearer meditation approaches to art, the better it is likely to be. Since expression and meaning are inseparable, skill in expression is bound to raise the quality of meditation.

Some works of creation, since they are done with the hands, leave the mind free. Would they not be enriched by an accompanying meditation?

As I plant a row of peas in the spring, I like to feel my oneness with earth and sun and seed. The earth has a live, warm smell as I lay it open; it awaits the seed. The seed has a dry, wrinkled look. After months of inertness, it longs for the soil. Though it seems dead, yet it is ready to spring into life. But they both need my hand—the soil and the seed. It is I who bring them together: and am I not doing the work of the divine creator? So the sun warms me, and the wind cools me as I squat upon the earth, placing seed that I am helpless to help once the dirt has been patted over them. My powers as an instrument are limited, but nature's power is as infinite as it is mysterious. To this infinity and this mystery I have to leave the seeds. But there will be peas in June. There always have been.

BEAUTY, THE DIVINE PLAY

But what is this beauty upon which the arts are based, and of which they are particular reflections?

90

Plato felt that man's love of beauty came from that divine part of him which perceived the soul's intrinsic nature and which desired to produce works that would mirror the divine creation. Beauty fosters our re-creation of ourselves in the image of divinity; it is the urge to reproduce the divinity we sense in ourselves.

Plotinus, building on Plato, said that when we long for beauty we are really longing for home—for goodness, for truth, for God. One might say that beauty is our symbol of the good, or that aspect of the divine creation that appeals to our senses and draws us up towards a knowledge of the divine. In medieval thought the ladder of beauty led upward from the physical to the spiritual, ending in union with the unity that is God.

Even Joseph Addison, as late as the eighteenth century, could say: "The Supreme Author of our being . . . has framed us so that we naturally delight in the great, the new, the beautiful. . . . Finally he has made us find the world in general beautiful so that we cannot behold His works with coldness or indifference." [2] Beauty is a kind of spur to hurry us toward the divine.

Edmund Burke saw that "beauty demands no assistance from our reasoning; even the will is unconcerned; the appearance of beauty as effectually causes some degree of love in us as the application of ice or fire produces the ideas of heat or cold. . . . I call beauty a social quality; for where women and men . . . give us a sense of joy and pleasure in beholding them . . . they inspire us with sentiments of tenderness and affection toward their persons; we like to have them near us." [3] Burke then divided beauty into three sorts: sympathy, such as we feel when watching a tragedy; imitation, which explains our interest in painting or poetry; and emulation, which we feel for the sublime.

The classical idea was that beauty provided a balance between sense and intellect in such a way as to preserve their independ-

[2] "The Spectator," no. 412.
[3] *A Philosophical Inquiry into the Origin of Our Ideas of the Sublime and Beautiful,* Part III, Sec. 2 and Part I, Sec. 10.

ence. But the romantics wiped out this distinction altogether. The romantic imagination was forever transforming the particular item of beauty into a symbol of transcendental beauty, as Wordsworth's skylark was true to the kindred points of heaven and home.

As late as the nineteenth century, Christian Weisse saw beauty as the emblem of liberty which God had engraved upon all creation and through which the mind perceived the infinite variety of the divine.

Whatever the theory of beauty—and this is no place to pursue all the ingenious ideas that have been wrapped around this thing we immediately know when we sense it—there seems to be no way of analyzing it that satisfactorily explains the direct impact beauty itself has upon us and the certainty with which we recognize it. The explanation of beauty really rests in our recognition of it. To say that beauty is that which we perceive to be beautiful gets us nowhere. But esthetics has never really solved the mystery.

Clearly, then, beauty is something both within and beyond us —within, so far as we surely know it when we see it; beyond, because we feel that every item of beauty is a symbol or an instance of some deeper, more permanent beauty we can never grasp. As much as anything, beauty is the divine play. In the Hindu view, the creator god made all things at play, out of his bountiful creativeness. Human play—the making of poems, pictures, embroidered rugs, decorated pottery—partakes of that same quality. God need not have made things beautiful, any more than man needs to decorate his pottery or his dwelling. That something extra, given out of love, out of sheer exuberance of creativeness, out of delight, is beauty. So beauty always ends in love. But how can one separate love from creativeness, or creativeness from beauty? And how but by meditation can one understand and respond to this divine union?

7

SCIENCE, MEDITATION,
WORLD RELIGION

ART displays one form of imagination, science another. Art deals with experience in one way, science in another. But imagination and a direct dealing with experience are common bonds. Good artists, good scientists have mastered the art of meditation whether they know it or not. Consequently, we can learn from them how to better our own meditation.

"Every creative act—in science, art or religion involves . . . a new innocence of perception liberated from the cataract of accepted beliefs." So writes Arthur Koestler in *The Sleepwalkers*. Innocence, wonder, imagination—these belong to the scientist (not the mere technician) as to the artist. Delight in the pursuit of truth, the scientist's goal, may not in the end be very different from the artist's search for beauty.

"Euclid alone has looked on Beauty bare," wrote Edna Millay. In this spirit of innocence the true scientist looks at the world with young eyes, as if he were seeing it for the first time. He is delighted if this new vision opens the way to a theory or a discovery which upsets the very "laws" of science on which he has been raised, and so are his colleagues. Truth is the goal, not any completed blueprint of the universe. And since the history of science makes it very clear that today's truth is tomorrow's error, the scientist has every reason to keep hunting amid the facts and evidences of the material world for new and better explanations of its phenomena.

Meditation: The Inward Art

This uncertainty which undergirds experience and our understanding of it—this necessity for constantly rephrasing and redrawing our picture of truth—is a healthy thing. It keeps us on our toes and gives us an ever new picture of our universe. Each discovery discloses new marvels, new possibilities. Yesterday gravitation explained the celestial movements, today relativity, tomorrow something else. Until the seventeenth century, men had no idea of the way the blood circulated, and were content with a medical theory which accounted for their ills on the basis of four "humors."

Uncertainty is a necessary and welcome attribute of our condition. The scientific method involves questioning everything until a point is reached where doubt cannot exist. But tomorrow this too may be questioned and corrected.

Like science, religion has also been a constant seeker for truth. Yet religions—those institutions which harden into stone —have forever kept trying to build their fences on a line marked out by the past, forbidding the faithful to march or even to look beyond. No wonder so many have left these institutions.

The most vital religion would be one which had no creed at all, but which encouraged its members to seek the truth with all their hearts and souls and minds, and to report these truths so that all might benefit, as in the case of science. Then what a religious flowering we should have!

The only religion that can be true is the one based upon experience—one that is felt within, which is precisely where all great religious leaders have told us to look. We should begin, like the scientist, with a desire for truth and a knowledge of the disciplines by which it is pursued. Like the artist, we should keep our imaginations alert. Openness to truth and to beauty are not professional prerogatives. They are essential to the religious seeker, the meditator.

Near the beginning of Shaw's *Saint Joan,* Joan is being questioned about her voices. "I hear voices telling me what to do," she says. "They come from God."

"They come from your imagination," says Robert de Baudricourt.

"Of course," Joan replies. "That is how the messages of God come to us." [1]

THE CHEMISTRY OF THOUGHT

One of the roads science has recently taken leads to the chemistry of thought itself. The brain contains two main types of cells, neurons and glial cells. The smaller glial cells stick to the neurons, which increase their content of enzyme proteins under stimulation, with a corresponding drop in the glials. Information, in the form of protein formed in the neuron, becomes an electrochemical impulse which is transmitted to nearby neurons. Memory and reasoning are determined by the way the neuron alters the proteins it forms. These modified proteins are the chemical equivalent of thoughts. Ribonucleic acid is imprinted in millions of cells, in patterns resembling the holes in an IBM card. Recognition—of a musical note, a face, a fact—is actually a chemical response between cells which have the same pattern. Since a human brain has ten billion neurons, the number of permutations is vast. Each neuron, moreover, may take part simultaneously in many networks.

Another study has opened up the possibility of two electric currents in the brain. One is the primordial, primitive guidance system operating as a direct current. The other consists of alternating impulses which accompany activity in the nerves. The theory is that evolution gradually produced the quicker and more responsive alternating current, but that underneath it, the ancient data transmission system still directs us, and the ability of a nerve to convey sense and motor impulses still depends on the primordial current.

The two currents remind one of the underlying time signature of music as it supports the varying rhythms of the composition,

[1] *Saint Joan*, Penguin Books, Baltimore, 1951, p. 77.

or of metre and rhythm in poetry.

Other studies have also indicated that men may indeed be affected by geomagnetic forces. "A relationship does exist between the incidence of psychiatric disturbances in the human population and some geophysical parameter coupled with the magnetic field." [2]

Further research will no doubt clarify this fascinating inquiry into the brain's operation. But the exercise of even a little imagination will suggest that since the functioning of the brain is electrochemical, and since cosmic radiations can affect us, God may turn out to be an electric transmission system who gives us an initial but lifelong charge, and who occasionally recharges us from outer space!

Even as I say this humorously, I do mean seriously to suggest that as science explores the electrochemical bases of thought and the essentially electrical impulses that constitute and distinguish matter, we may be on the threshold of great discoveries that will make man's relation to the universe clearer. As material turns out to be more and more immaterial—a matter of impulses and motions of submicroscopic particles—the difference between "material" and "spiritual" narrows. The difference between "personal" and "impersonal" narrows too. Science and religion may suddenly discover that they are talking about the same thing. Those chemical impulses in the brain—how were they originally triggered? What keeps them so amazingly and complicatedly on course?

While lifeless matter moves towards more randomness and the dispersal of matter and energy, as the physicists tell us our expanding universe is doing, sentient life is building a system of ever greater complexity from its chaotic environment, thus decreasing the randomness of matter. What is the source of this organizing principle and its opposition to the vast outward movement of the galaxies?

[2] For Swedish biologist Holger Hyden's work on neurons, see *Time,* Feb. 10, 1961, p. 47. For the two currents and geomagnetism, *Saturday Review,* Feb. 3, 1962.

The older theory of atomic structure saw the nucleus as a positive charge which held the electrons in their orbits as they circulated around it. The new theory sees the motion within the atom as ripples and waves which fill its entire space, making music as they move. Yes, music! By converting the frequency downward to the audible range, this music can actually be heard. I have even heard a scientist play a composition on the piano which was based on this atomic music. Science, the authority on the material world, is now saying that the true nature of matter and of the universe may reside in this music. Quite a change from the mechanistic theories of yesterday! And how dramatically it reinforces Keats'

Heard melodies are sweet, but those unheard are sweeter!

THE SEARCH FOR TRUTH

Long ago William James pointed out that the scientist's belief in truth, in the ability of his experiments to discover truth, and in the ability of the mind to recognize truth, are really based on an undemonstrable faith, just as much as religion is. "There is indeed nothing which someone has not thought absolutely true, while his neighbor deemed it absolutely false." [3] Science also has to guess, and would be far less advanced than it is if the passion to confirm a wild hunch had been ignored. And science still has to depend on consciousness—a thing about which it knows very little and whose reliability it has to take on faith.

Science has its own shortcomings. As Paul Tillich has pointed out, it gives us means without ends. Science, taking root in the Renaissance with its subjugation of nature, and in the Reformation with its aim of subjecting the world and mankind to the kingdom of God, lost its contact with the older ideals of self-realization and self-correction. Technique has become an end in itself. We now manipulate not only things but men, through social "engineering." Yet we have not decided who should con-

[3] *The Will to Believe,* New York, 1896, p. 16.

trol such manipulating, nor for what ends.

But along the frontier of science, a very different atmosphere is apparent. Physicists, listening to the music of the atom, are acquiring an entirely different idea and attitude about matter. Photons and electrons are individuals when regarded as particles, but members of an organization when regarded within the wave picture, where they lose their individuality. So, suggests James Jeans in *Physics and Philosophy,* space and time are inhabited by individuals, but as we progress from the world of phenomena towards reality, individuality is replaced by community. Passing beyond space and time, men may possibly form the ingredients of a continuous stream of life. This comes close to the religious idea of the one, the all, into which all is gathered.

On its speculative edge, then, science becomes more and more hospitable to the ageless spiritual insights of man. As Edmund Sinnott remarks in *Two Roads to Truth,* the two great strains of Western culture, intellectual and spiritual, once united, have split to the damage of both. Religion and science are not incompatible; they need to be reunited.

But on whose terms?

William James, summarizing the characteristics of the religious life, listed five basic qualities: 1, that the visible world is part of a spiritual universe from which it draws its chief significance; 2, that union with that higher universe is our true end; 3, that prayer or inner communion with the spirit of it is a process wherein work is done and spiritual energy flows in to affect the phenomenal world; 4, that new zest adds itself like a gift to life; 5, that there comes an assurance of safety and a temper of peace and love.[4]

Accepting religious experience as true, he concluded: "We and God have business with each other; and in opening ourselves to his influence our deepest destiny is fulfilled." The nature of this higher reality, this something larger than ourselves, remains an unanswered question just as ultimate truth remains beyond

[4] *The Varieties of Religious Experience.*

the grasp of the scientist, and always will.

What sort of a God would he be about whom we felt that we already knew everything? God is real *because* he is beyond us—because he is the symbol of that truth and goodness and beauty we surmise in our hearts and search for all our lives, and never fully know. Let us if we like call God the supreme hypothesis, the unreached goal of all our searching, and at the same time the source of that within us which knows that truth, beauty and goodness exist.

The goal of art, of science, of religion is enlargement. The more we fix upon goals rather than particular instances of behavior, the clearer it is that they are walking the same path, or at least climbing the same mountain.

WHAT IS TRUE RELIGION?

What, then, is true religion?

To some, God is a person, made manifest in Jesus of Nazareth, in Gautama the Buddha, in Krishna or Ram or Shiva. To others, God is Nature regarded as a manifestation of creative force. To some, God is chiefly or wholly manifest in man.

True religion is the one a man can accept honestly for himself, without surrendering his integrity, his ability to believe.

Nor is it necessary to accept the idea of a personal God, though as science progresses from a mechanistic to a musical concept of the universe, the personal or spiritual concept is going to grow easier for us to accept. For who can doubt, really, that a view of the universe not restricted by our human limitations would disclose that reality as it is intimated to us through truth, beauty and goodness—through art, science and religion—would turn out to be a unity far more perfect than we can imagine, and far more beautiful?

Meditation, if faithfully practised, will at least open the way to such a wider view, for simply to conceive it is to have a partial glimpse of it. And meditation will foster that sense of unity which brings peace and a wider perspective on the self.

Sixty years ago Richard Bucke proposed a theory of personal evolution which he called *Cosmic Consciousness*. It was his belief that man had not yet reached his fullest development, though a few rare individuals had demonstrated a capacity for love, understanding, and "cosmic consciousness" which all men would some day share, vastly advancing our creative powers and opening the possibility of a social order beyond anything we now know. Ten years ago Charles Francis Potter, bringing Bucke up to date, in *Creative Personality* presented additional evidence that we are in the midst of such an evolutionary period.

If this is so, we should find the springs of it within ourselves through meditation. Through well-directed meditation we can foster that within which is ready to lift us to such a stage.

RELIGION AND THEOLOGY

During a voyage to London in 1840 Lucretia Mott, Quaker worker for equal rights for women as well as for Negroes, said to Elizabeth Stanton:

"There is a broad distinction between religion and theology. The one is a natural human experience, common to all well-organized minds. The other is a system of speculation about the unseen, the unknowable, which the human mind has no power to grasp or explain; and these speculations vary with every sect, age, and type of civilization. No one knows any more of what lies beyond our sphere of action than thou and I; and we know nothing." [5]

If every religion would take these words to heart, what a freshening of the spirit mankind would experience! For theology is speculation, but religion is experience.

[5] Quoted in Charles and Mary Beard, *The American Spirit*, New York, 1942, p. 207.

But isn't meditation encouraging theology by encouraging speculation?

Not at all. The purpose of meditation is not to generate new dogmas or to warm over old ones, but to put the whole self in touch with the source of life, to cut through the dead tissue of doctrine, cliché, and notions accepted uncritically, awakening that of God in every man. We try to tune in on that music of the atom—not to build theories about it, but to experience it.

THE COURSE OF TRUE RELIGION

The major religions have begun with the teachings of a prophet whose message was so plain and whose voice so clear that men gathered around him as around a spring of fresh water. Then the message, spread by enthusiasts, grows because of its apparent truth and healing power. Men everywhere, perhaps simple men best of all, recognize and respond to its truth.

But then, after the death of the teacher, a terrible thing begins to happen. The simple teaching hardens into dogma, is asserted to be the one acceptable truth, and is fastened like chains upon all within its power.

This has been the melancholy history of most religions. First the plain truth—Jesus' message of love and forgiveness, Buddha's way of attaining peace by overcoming desire—ringingly declared, recognized and welcomed. Then the slow strangulation of that truth by an institution which ritualizes, dogmatizes and encumbers it to death as it makes one hopeless attempt after another to shore up a building that has been falsely built. On the notion that an assertion once made must never be changed. On authority instead of experience. On external imposition instead of internal convincement. On creed rather than method.

Meanwhile the truth remains. Those who go back to the original teacher can easily find it in the words of Jesus, Buddha or Mohammed. And what do they all say? The kingdom of God is

101

within you—not in an imagined heaven, not in images or relics or churches or temples, or in saints or priests or in books. Religion is experience. It must be felt. It must be seized. The only true religion is the one which is true for you.

All the great religious teachers urge us to realize the divine in this life, through purity, self-control, and the recognition of its presence within us. That is the purpose of meditation. The higher we climb the mountain in our religious search, the more clearly we see that all paths come out upon the same summit.

Wrote John Woolman, the American Quaker who sought spiritual unity with Negro and Indian, in *Some Considerations on the Keeping of Negroes* which Benjamin Franklin published in 1762:

"There is a Principle which is pure, placed in the human Mind, which in different Places and Ages hath had different Names: it is, however, pure, and proceeds from God. It is deep, and inward, confined to no Forms of Religion nor excluded from any, where the Heart stands in perfect Sincerity. In whomsoever this takes Root and grows, of what Nation soever, they become Brethren, in the best Sense of the Expression."

Every major faith has some branch or group which retains and practises this pure, uncontroversial religion and which welcomes as brothers those of every culture who have also seen this universal light. It is a method, not a creed—a courageous, honest willingness to doubt, to move forward as truth opens, to declare only that which is firmly experienced. It is the way of the mystic; it is meditative, it is experiential; it is bound to good works because the oneness the individual feels with the divine embraces all men.

A MODERN FAITH

In *Religion and the Rise of Scepticism,* Franklin Baumer predicts that a new faith is taking shape in our time. It will be a layman's faith rather than a priest's; every man will have a responsibility for it. It will creatively combine skepticism with religion. It will recognize many equally valid forms of the one universal religious impulse. It will eschew dogmatizing. It will rely upon religious experience as expressed in the myth or symbol which has meaning for the particular seeker instead of forcing a common symbolism upon all.

This, exactly, is where meditation leads.

Meditation need not and should not lead the seeker away from the faith to which he already belongs. It should strengthen him as a member of that company, deepen his insights, make the particular service or ritual of his faith more meaningful to him, and help him to understand its symbols.

Plans are being made to build in Washington a Temple of Understanding with six wings for the major living religions— Hinduism, Islam, Buddhism, Confucianism, Judaism and Christianity. It will provide a rare opportunity for men of all religions to understand one another and for seekers to discover what is good in all.

I hope no one expects it to lead toward one universal religion. There is a lot of nonsense talked nowadays about uniting all Christian churches in one. So long as the effort is based upon a creed, upon an authority which tells its members what to believe, the union will be temporary. Men, thank God, are of so many kinds and dispositions and temperaments that they need variety in religion as they need variety in food, housing, jobs, and friends. Yet in this variety they will find the unity of faith itself. Religions do not need a union; they need a federation.

One of the chief difficulties in the way of understanding is the name we give to the divine. The Hindus alone have hundreds of names for it, from the threefold Brahma, Shiva and Vishnu or the all-embracing Om to various snake gods and divine reincarnations. We Christians are not quite sure whether God is one or three, or whether Jesus is man or God, or both. The Jews and Muslims are clearest about the oneness of God, but they are also clear that he is a God only for those who accept Jewish or Muslim laws. So we shut ourselves off from each other.

Let us for a moment meditate about the divine name. If we seek a word which would be universally acceptable, what comes to mind?

The Divine. The Radiant One. The Creator. The Enlightener. The Light. The Inward Light. The Source. The Universal Radiance. The True Vine. The Author of truth, beauty and the good. The Maker. The Universal Harmony. The Eternal. The Father of life.

It is in the nature of religion and of man that the nature of the divine can never be known. But that need not discourage us. We do not know the secret of life either, yet we know the motions of love by which to give ourselves children. So we know the devotions of service and of meditation by which we reach towards the divine. If anything, we are too timid in conceiving the divine. We tend to remain within the boundaries of the faith and the culture we were born to. But God is not so limited. We should be bold to make the grand assertion that God is that and that and that—whatever Muslim or Sikh or Hindu or Jew or Christian has found Him to be. Only then shall we come close to the truth.

Religion is not the opiate of the people as Marx thought; only a cynical establishment is that. Religion is the one true stimulant —the goad which keeps man searching for the true, the beautiful, the good. Perhaps religion is only that: a seeking. A longing for some felt home in an unknown land.

The way to seek is to meditate. Meditation is therefore a moral force, enlarging mankind. We shall never achieve the final enlargement. This is man's limitation and his salvation. There will always be another hill to climb, another evil to overcome, another mystery to search, another glory to assimilate.

So we shall still need meditation.

8

HINDU MEDITATION AND YOGA

INDIA has experimented with meditation for thousands of years. But it is impossible to describe Hindu methods without first touching briefly on the religious principles they rest upon.

In Hindu thought, God alone is real. Brahman, the supreme reality, whose name means something like "the great one," is being, awareness and bliss (*sat, chit, ananda*), and the ground of man's being, man's awareness, man's bliss.

"The man consists of his faith," says Krishna in the Bhagavad-Gita. "He is verily what his faith is." (A good starting point for a meditation.)

If God is the sole reality and man is what his faith makes him, it follows that man's greatest work is to reach God, realize God. It is not surprising therefore that the Hindus above all religious practitioners have devoted themselves to meditation and to ways of perfecting it.

The Hindu concept of the divine is a grand one. The manifested universe forms only a minute portion of his being. For the most part he is unmanifested and immortal. But he manifests himself in many ways.

"It is one and the same Savior," said Ramakrishna, "that, having plunged into the ocean of life, rises up in one place and is known as Krishna, and diving down again rises in another place and is known as Christ."

Yet from another Hindu point of view the whole universe is

one vast temptation—it is Maya, the divine illusion, the manifest aspect of the divine which man can see but which is the least part of the divine whole.

Hindu thought is fascinated both by unity and variety. Nowhere have men developed a stronger sense of the unity of life, yet paradoxically it is in India that religion exhibits the greatest variety. God is known by hundreds of names and through many manifestations and forms. Temples are raised to each of the many gods, and are adorned with a bewildering profusion of forms to illustrate the stories from the sacred books or the apparent enjoyment the divine ones take in music, dance and sex.

How, then, can God be one, if he is many?

To the religious Hindu, God is everything. He can manifest himself in nature or in man. He can appear at various ages or at any moment in a sainted person. One need not live in India very long to see that the divine is taken for granted as an ever-present element in life.

"Indians think there's a bit of God in every man," Nehru once said to me. It is therefore a proof of God's presence that he manifests himself in many shapes and ways. The idea that there must have been only one incarnation of God in Jesus strikes them as strange and niggardly. Why should God have appeared only once in man? Is he not appearing repeatedly?

The manifold, therefore, is a proof of the one. God's many appearances are continuing proof of his existence, and there is nothing basically opposite about the one and the many as we have been taught. The many make the one manifest. Variety is the drama through which we perceive unity. God has spread this magnificent pageant before us so that we may know his power —his being, his awareness, his bliss. But all this glory we see is but the scraps of his oneness, his perfection.

The divine is not only around us; it is within us. It is the ground of our being. We are in God. Says Krishna: "I am not in them, but they are in Me." God is the all of which man is a part.

Gandhi loved the verse from the *Ishopanishad* which goes:

"All this, whatsoever moves on earth, is pervaded by the Lord. When thou has surrendered all this, then thou mayst enjoy."

All men are inherently divine, but they come into their heritage when they recognize it, identify themselves with it, and carry out the divine will.

Krishna again: "Those who worship Me and meditate on Me without any other thought, to these ever steadfast devotees, I secure safety and supply all their needs. . . . Whatever thou doest, whatever thou eatest, whatever thou offerest as oblation, whatever thou givest and the austerities thou performest, O son of Kunti, do that as an offering to me. . . . Those who worship me with devotion, they are in Me and I am in them."

This leads to the central paradox of Hindu religious thought and the basis of its meditation. Indeed, it suggests the only basis for meditation:

"Thou art that." Atman, the individual soul, is a part of Brahman, the universal soul. Therefore the self in one is the self in all, and the divine in one is the divine in all. The individual self is like a glass immersed in water—both filled and surrounded by one divine essence. In the world of religious significance the light, the lighter, and the lighted are one.

A beautiful passage in the *Chandogya Upanishad* makes the point with just that touch of poetry which is needed to light it up.

"The intelligent, whose body is spirit, whose form is light, whose thoughts are true, whose nature is like ether, from whom all works, all desires, all sweet odors and tastes proceed; he who embraces all this, who never speaks, and is never surprised,

"He is my self within the heart, smaller than a corn of rice, smaller than a corn of barley, smaller than a mustard seed, smaller than a canary seed or the kernel of a canary seed. He also is my self within the heart, greater than the earth, greater than the sky, greater than heaven, greater than all these worlds.

"He from whom all works, all desires, all sweet odors and tastes proceed, who embraces all this, who never speaks and who is never surprised, he, my self within the heart, is that Brahman."

Atman, the individual soul, and Brahman, the world soul, are one. This is the central assertion to which Hindu thought keeps returning. "Thou art that."

Western thought, with its compulsion to analyze and separate, has seen God as immanent and transcendent, but has not generally been at ease about bringing the two attributes together, except of course through the incarnation of the divine spirit in Jesus as the Son of God. Hinduism, with a grand surmise and an intuitive certainty, sees immanence and transcendence as complementary attributes of the divine.

And how is this presence made known?

There is but one instrument—the mind of man. And for thousands of years Hindu thinkers and holy men have labored to perfect the instrument so that it may respond, like a seismograph, to the gentlest tremors. Only through the mind of man can the divine be known. Meditation is therefore the main activity of the religious individual.

The world with all its temptations, since it is Maya, or illusion (yet paradoxically also a manifestation of the divine), raises a wall between self and spirit that must come down. The world of matter must be surmounted to get at the pure spirit which is the true nature of reality. Hindu sages therefore place a good deal of emphasis upon self-control. The earnest seeker will control all his appetites—not only for food and sex, but for comfort and all sorts of pleasures that delude the senses and draw the self away from its principal business—the realization of that breath of life which is spirit.

YOGA EXERCISES

Since the body may tempt one away from the main business, its tendencies are to be controlled by exercises and purification. This is the basis of the famous Yoga exercises.

A fear of pollution runs through Hindu thought, and is answered by an emphasis on acts or rituals of purification. Some of these may take an extreme form, as in the vigorous scouring of the mouth and throat, the passing of a string up through the nostril and out of the mouth, or the emptying of the stomach by swallowing yards of thin cloth or taking in and regurgitating water. Gandhi used to brush his teeth for fifteen minutes each morning, and spend twenty minutes at his bath. Such practices, bound up as they are in a rather unscientific conception of the body and its functions, need not alienate us from the rest of Yoga.

Anyone attempting to follow all the recommended practices of Yoga—the postures, the exercises, the breathing, the techniques for concentration, the *mantras* (sacred chants), and the prolonged periods of concentration leading through meditation to *samadhi*—the merging into the universal being—would have to spend all his time at it. But it is also possible to plan a simple set of exercises quite adequate to the needs of the inquirer who would like to attempt meditation after the Yoga manner.

For more than a year I have done Yoga exercises each morning as soon as I wake up. I claim no great benefits from them. I am not clear that they raise the quality of meditation. A lot of nonsense has been written about Yoga, and many inflated claims made about the benefits arising from Yoga exercise. Anyway, they do no harm unless too much is attempted, and they may have a certain calming influence. At worst, they are good for limbering relaxed or flabby or stiff muscles, and make an appropriate entrance to meditation, Yoga style.

109

Here, then, is a plan for about twelve to fifteen minutes. It is best to wear little or no clothing.

1. Stand with back somewhat bent and hands on thighs. Nearly empty your lungs. Draw in and then release the abdomen fifteen or twenty times before resting. (You may have to begin at ten or twelve.) Then repeat the cycle until you have done three cycles of twenty each.

2. Lie flat on a rug or carpeted floor. Raise your legs and body slowly above your head until as much as possible of your back is off the floor. Support yourself in this position by placing your hands under your hips, bracing your elbows on the floor. Hold the position for a minute or more. Rest quietly and prone for about 15 seconds. All of these positions should be assumed slowly and in a relaxed manner, gradually stretching to the final state. To gauge the time, count your breaths. 18 or 20 probably make a minute. You may also say a word with each breath, using the Lord's Prayer or a favorite poem.

3. Raise your feet up over your head and stretch them behind as far as they will go. A true yogi can touch the floor behind his head, but you needn't expect to do that! Hold the position for a minute. Then rest.

4. Lie on your stomach. Place your hands by your chest and slowly raise yourself, using the back muscles as much as possible, until your body from the knees up is arched as far as possible from the floor. Fix your gaze on the ceiling. Hold it for a minute, then rest.

5. Lying on your back, raise your torso slowly and bend forward until you grip your toes with your hands, stretching your back as much as possible and keeping your legs as flat to the floor as you can. Stay in this position for a minute, then rest.

6. Turn onto your stomach again. Gradually raise your torso from the floor, and reach out behind until you have grasped your ankles with your hands. Remain in this position as long as you can, arching your head upward as much as possible so that your

body takes the shape of a bow, only the hips resting on the floor. You will not be able to retain this position very long at first, but within a week or two will be able to manage a minute. You will also probably want a longer rest after this one!

7. Sit up, crossing your legs in front of you. Let your head drop a bit so that you are looking at your belly. Draw the abdomen in with a sudden quick pull so that the breath is forced out. Do this ten times, as quickly as convenient, then rest. Do four cycles in all, then rest. You may at first find this difficult, but it is rapidly learned. The rhythm seems to come more easily if you watch the motions of the abdomen. Work up to four cycles of thirty each.

8. Still in the sitting position, draw a middling deep breath and expel it by drawing the abdomen in and up. Do this twelve times. Then close the right nostril with a finger and fill the lungs slowly and steadily through the left. When they are really full, expel the air slowly and steadily by closing the left nostril and letting the air out through the right. Repeat the cycle of twelve breaths, then close the left nostril, breathe in deeply through the right, and exhale slowly and steadily through the left. Rest.

9. Still sitting, draw a full draught of air in through both nostrils, making the throat constricted so that you hear the air as it passes. Then drop your chin to your chest and hold the air as long as you comfortably can. Let it out very slowly, as if you could feel it draining out all the way from your toes. Repeat the cycle once.

10. Lie down straight and flat on the carpet, letting your arms rest along your sides. Relax completely, beginning with the scalp and ending with your soles, consciously relaxing each muscle as you move mentally down the body. Remain in this completely relaxed state for two or three minutes.

You are now ready to begin a period of ten to fifteen minutes of meditation. But before we can proceed with this, several things have to be said.

As to the exercises, never force or strain yourself. It may take several weeks to accomplish fully even the very simple and easy course described above. The whole purpose of the exercises is, or should be, to make meditation easier. The bending and stretching exercises are undertaken so that the body can be taught to remain motionless for long periods, without intruding upon the meditating mind. The breathing exercises are intended to give the meditator complete control of breathing so that he can again forget the body—place it behind him, so to speak, as he goes into deep meditation. In Hindu thought the breath is almost synonymous with spirit and therefore gets special attention.

We are not concerned here with the claims that yogis can suspend their breathing, even suppress the heartbeat, and can be buried alive and dug up. Nor do we care about the bodily contortions, such as the moving of the muscles first on one side, then the other. Hinduism with its strong ascetic strain sometimes assumes that mortifying the body assures spiritual advancement. Thousands of Hindus have been willing to devote their whole lives to austere regimens of exercising and fasting in the confident assumption that this would increase their spiritual powers. Gandhi was only expressing a deeply etched pattern of Indian living when he gave up sexual intercourse, reduced his diet to one just sufficient to sustain life, slept little, and made the times of prayer and meditation the important occasions of his day.

In addition to a rigid control over bodily appetites and pleasures, the true Hindu or yogi also believes that a strict moral code must be followed before the aspirant can achieve spiritual results.

The yogi is instructed to abstain from injury to life, lying, stealing, sensuality and greed, and to practise cleanliness, contentment, self-control, studiousness and contemplation of the divine. Kindness, truth, and nonviolence are among the most important virtues. It was upon these that Gandhi built his famous doctrine, or working plan, of *satyagraha,* usually translated as "truth-force," and with it brought about India's independence. Such is the power of moral force in India.

THE BASIS OF YOGA MEDITATION

The teachings of Hinduism come close to that of Jesus when he said, "He that loseth his life for my sake shall find it." (Matthew 10:39.) Behind the idea of rigid self-control even to the point of self-negation and mortification is the sense that the real world lies beyond the impermanent physical world, the world of illusion. The real world is one of spirit, and to reach it one must free himself of desire for wealth or sex or comfort. There is no peace for man until he finds his way through all this to the state of changeless reality known as Nirvana. This can be reached only by renunciation and meditation which will liberate the self for the discovery of its oneness with Brahman. "Thou art that." When the ego is annihilated, man is freed not only from the narrow self and from the lure of Maya, the illusory world, but also from the restricting and false knowledge his intellect imposes upon reality—through such ideas as duality and relativity, good and evil.

The end of Yoga meditation, therefore, is nothing less than to reunite the individual self with the world self, Atman with Brahman, this with that—with the beyond that lies within. By control of the mind through self-discipline, the purity of the divine that lies within the self can be recaptured.

The word *Yoga* itself comes from the same root as "yoke"—to bind.

Yoga meditation therefore involves a number of steps.

First, the practice of the virtues and abstentions named above.

Second, the exercises which quiet the body and breath.

Third, gathering the mind from the senses which distract and enthrall it, by concentrating on some object or idea (*pratyahara*).

Fourth, meditation upon the object or idea in such a way as to concentrate upon the divine (*dhyana*).

Fifth, absorption of the self in the universal (*samadhi*). This comes about through the discovery of a self which is separated from body and mind, pure and perfect.

Nothing can clarify the Yoga approach better than a few verses from the most admired of all Hindu sacred works, the Bhagavad-Gita. In addition to its summing up of Hindu ethical teaching as the Sermon on the Mount summarizes the Christian, it is also a little treatise on Yoga. Lord Krishna is the speaker.

"When a man is satisfied in the Self alone and has completely cast out all desires from the mind, then he is said to be of steady wisdom."

"He who is free from all attachment and neither rejoices on receiving good nor is vexed on receiving evil, his wisdom is well-established."

"Nothing indeed in this world purifies like wisdom. He who is perfected by Yoga, finds it in time within himself by himself."

"One who is devoted to Yoga, of purified mind, self-subjugated and a master of the senses, realizes his Self as the Self of all beings."

"He whose joy is within, whose pleasure is within, and whose light is within, that Yogi, being well-established in Brahman, attains to absolute freedom."

"He whose heart is steadfastly engaged in Yoga, looks everywhere with the eyes of equality, seeing the Self in all beings and all beings in the Self."

"He who, being established in unity, worships Me dwelling in all beings, that Yogi, howsoever living, abides in Me."

Any one of these verses, or all of them in succession, would make starting points for meditation.

YOGA TECHNIQUES

We have now come to the point where we can begin meditation Yoga style, taking up at the point where we rested, relaxed, for several minutes after exercises.

Again assume the sitting posture, with legs crossed in front of you. The lotus position of meditation, with feet tucked up over the thighs, is beyond the competence of most Westerners. We don't seem to be made that way. Sitting with legs crossed comfortably in front of you is just as good. The whole point in Yoga meditation is to make the body at ease while still alert, so that it can be ignored and forgotten. If you cannot manage this with legs crossed while in the middle of the floor, sit close to a wall where you can get some support for the back. If you are still uncomfortable, and find it unlikely that you can learn to be at ease this way, use a comfortable chair. Yoga insists that the back should be erect. The reasons given are esoteric, having to do with the "serpent" that is supposed to lie within spinal cord and brain, but I suspect the real reason is that in India's hot climate it is too easy to fall asleep if you lie down.

"Being seated there," Krishna advises Arjuna, "making the mind one-pointed and subduing the activities of mind and senses, let him practise Yoga for self-purification.

"Let him hold his body, head and neck erect and motionless, fixing the gaze on the tip of his nose, not looking around.

"Being serene-hearted and fearless, ever steadfast in the vow of *Brahmacharya* [sexual abstinence] and controlling the mind, let him sit steadfastly absorbed in thoughts of Me, regarding Me as his supreme goal.

"Thus ever keeping himself steadfast, the Yogi of subdued mind attains eternal peace and freedom, which abide in Me."

This is the beginning of Yoga meditation. Perhaps the important word is "one-pointed." Krishna has already explained this to Arjuna:

"The well-resolved mind is single and one-pointed; but the purposes of the irresolute mind are many-branched and endless."

To keep the mind from scurrying about is the first step in meditation, and many ways have been suggested.

115

Meditation: The Inward Art

1. Begin by merely observing the thoughts that flow unprompted through the mind. With practice, this flow can be very quickly turned off so that the mind can sink to a deeper level. But at first the flow must continue while you observe it, and without agitation let it go as you sometimes have to let the air out of a water line. After a while, interrupt the flow for a brief moment and a brief glimpse of the stillness which is your goal.

2. Seize upon an idea which flows by and use it for effective meditation, as previously suggested on page 21.

3. Concentrate upon an object which you have placed in a convenient position. It may be a flower, a picture, a vase, or some other object of beauty. Focus upon it, and if your mind tries to wander, bring it back. Examine it with all your powers of perception. Close your eyes and "see" the object with your inward eye, recalling all its details. Meditate upon the object—upon the significance of its form or shape or meaning. Concentrate upon its essence—the meaning of its being. See it next in the great stream of creation of which it is a part. See it in its relation to yourself. See both self and object as beings joined by the great stream of being. Enter into it, by virtue of this common, uniting stream until you become one with it.

4. Concentrate in similar fashion upon a light. Begin with a shaded electric light or candle, or with star or moon, and keep the gaze unwaveringly upon it, emptying the mind of everything else. The mind should become illumined, so that when you close your eyes, your whole mind will seem full of light. When the light grows inward so that light, source and viewer become as one, *dhyana* is achieved. Yogis say that such a period of realization should last for twelve seconds. If this state can be maintained for twelve times twelve seconds, *samadhi* is attained—a state in which the self has become absorbed beyond self-consciousness into the universal consciousness. More of this later.

5. Make your concentration upon a sound. Everyone has had the experience of being soothed by the sound of a brook, a water-

fall, the lapping of waves along a lake or ocean shore. If you have the opportunity, meditate in the presence of one of these sounds, or to the sound of rain or wind in trees. Perhaps even the distant roar of city traffic would do as a modern substitute! Or the tick of a clock. Or you can concentrate upon your memory of such a sound, until it becomes the epitome of all sounds, until you have thought of the music that is within the atom and can now be detected and transferred to audible sounds electronically, and of the oneness of all sound which, merging in infinity, will become one with the hearer.

6. A variety of this is to concentrate upon the effulgent light within the heart. This light, through concentration, will also grow until the self is absorbed through it into the infinite.

7. One may begin by meditation upon the divine glory as manifested in a holy personality—Jesus, Saint Francis, Brother Lawrence, Krishna, Ram, Buddha.

8. One may concentrate on making the mind void, shutting off senses, impressions, thoughts, active meditation. Even a few seconds of this emptiness is supposed to give an idea of the formless aspect of Brahman, usually beyond our grasp since we deal mostly in the finite which is but a minor aspect of the divine.

9. Meditate upon Brahman or the divine being as a boundless ocean, and imagine yourself swimming in it.

10. Think of your body as a vessel, your mind as pure water reflecting the sun of the divine presence.

11. Attempt Krishna's exercise of fixing the gaze on the tip of the nose, and contemplate the meaning of self.

12. Yogic exercises include lengthy patterns of repeated phrases, often around the word OM (symbol of the allness of Brahman including his formlessness). This sort of meditation is not likely to be popular in the West, but I will give a much shortened example.

Who am I?

I am not my physical body—Om, Om, Om, Om, Om
I am not the bodily senses—Om, etc.
Nor the objects perceived by the senses—
I am not the mind—
I am not the will—
I am Brahma the Creator—
I am Vishnu the Sustainer—
I am Shiva the Destroyer—
I am the God of gods—
I am the Light of lights—
I have no disease—
I have no fear, no lust, no anger—
I am the Supreme Brahman, immortal and changeless—
I am eternal and infinite—Om, Om, Om, Om, Om.

And so on. I have quoted but a small portion. The earnest student is counseled to repeat the whole formula over and over with intense feeling, as if the whole body and mind are full of the divine, and to keep it in mind throughout the day. Meditation is then recommended on the insignificance of the world we know—one of a million momentary bubbles in a timeless cosmic ocean. "But I am Brahman, whose nature is being, knowledge, bliss. Nothing can make me weak, and ephemeral things do not concern me. I am Supreme Spirit." Many Yoga teachers count on having pupils who will devote all or most of their time to Yoga, and the exercises they recommend show this. They count on tireless iteration and reiteration, hour after hour, day after day, year after year to achieve their ends—which is the chief reason why Westerners are not likely to become yogis.

13. Sit in a place where you can view the whole sky. The Oversoul, which is also yourself, is everywhere—nearer than the air that surrounds you, deeper than the farthest reaches of space, eternal, infinite and changeless. Yet nothing in the universe is apart from Brahman, which is also your own self. The power of the self is therefore infinite. But to realize it, one must live a

life of absolute simplicity and purity.

14. Choose a favorite passage, and then meditate upon it. Here are a few examples. The first is from Albert Schweitzer:

"The important thing is that we are part of life. We are born of other lives; we possess the capacities to bring still other lives into existence. . . . In the very fibres of our being, we bear within ourselves the fact of the solidarity of life."

From the Bhagavad-Gita:

"The Lord dwells in the heart of all beings, causing all beings to revolve, as if mounted on a wheel. . . . Take refuge in Him with all thy heart; through His grace thou shalt attain Supreme Peace and the Eternal Abode."

From the *Svetasvatara Upanishad:*

"Thou art woman, thou art man; thou art youth, thou art maiden; thou, as an old man, totterest along on thy staff; thou art born with thy face turned everywhere. . . .

"Know then nature is art, and the great Lord the maker; the whole world is filled with what are his members. . . .

"That god, the maker of all things, the great Self, always dwelling in the heart of man, is perceived by the heart, the soul, the mind;—they who know it become immortal."

15. Consider the essence of the inner self as rays of light rising up the backbone, and that the vital life rises in you.

16. Concentrate upon the mind that was before thought. Let the mind fill as with the essence of the breath until it showers from the top of the head as light.

17. Immerse yourself in a continuous sound, such as that of a waterfall, or of rain, or in the sound made by covering the ears.

18. Intone a sound, making it softer and softer until feeling deepens into the harmony of silence.

19. Imagine yourself surrounded and invaded by spirit until the whole universe becomes spirit.

20. Feel your whole body inundated with the oneness of universal essence.

21. Think of being and not-being, of thinking and not-thinking, of doing and not-doing. Then leave them all and *be*.

22. In a moment of joy, feel yourself to be permeated by it.

23. Become the taste of the food you are eating and be filled with it.

24. Catch yourself at the moment of sleep and discover being.

25. Look at a loved person or scene as if for the first time.

26. As you talk with a friend, feel his consciousness as your own and enter into him.

27. Think that as waves to water and as flames with fire, so we are a wave of the universal.[1]

Each of these suggestions is good for one or more meditative sessions. Try them all. Return to those you find most fruitful.

STAGES IN MEDITATION

We must now take a closer look at the stages of meditation as described by Hindu thinkers, who for thousands of years have turned their thoughts towards this, to them, most important of all human activities.

After performance of the exercises, the first step is *pratyahara,* that withdrawal of the senses which "cleanses" the mind and makes it ready for true meditation. We have described a number of methods designed to achieve this. Another way of defining *pratyahara* is the gathering and converging of the mind, at the will and command of the meditator, at one particular place. Perhaps there are really two stages here, but the Yoga literature does not separate them.

The next stage, *dharana,* is one of concentration—the one-pointedness so often mentioned in yogic thought. Once learned,

[1] 15–27 are adapted from ancient Sanskrit manuscripts in the possession of a Kashmiri monk, Lakshmanjoo, Englished by him and Paul Reps. See *Zen Flesh, Zen Bones,* Doubleday Anchor Book, 1961.

this power of fixing the mind upon a single object or idea is useful in every department of life.

Next comes *dhyana,* described as a state of concentration in which thought flows like oil from a vessel in a continuous stream toward the object, or in which the mind is able to hold itself upon the object of concentration without wavering.

Finally, when subject and object become one, the state of *samadhi* is achieved. Two stages are distinguished—the first, in which the thought of control still remains; the last, in which there is complete identification of thinker and thought, subject and object, Self and Absolute. The I ceases to exist apart from the all, and the tyranny of self, place, time and desire are overcome. Nothing is in the mind but the divine. The world is annihilated and only the disembodied self remains, absorbed into the divine.

Can anyone achieve this state? Probably not everyone. But possibly anyone who is normally intelligent and who takes religious experience seriously and is willing to have daily periods of meditation as part of the regular cycle of life.

Isn't it strange, once you think of it, that a man will feel debased and unkempt if he has to pass a day without washing, brushing his teeth and shaving, but thinks nothing of going for years without properly overhauling mind and spirit? The world would be transformed if everyone paid as much attention to his real as to his bodily self!

There remains one point about Yoga which ought to be included for the record though it verges upon the magic use of psychic powers and does not concern us here. By learning to concentrate the three high states of *dharana, dhyana* and *samadhi* (together called *samyama*) upon an object, unusual results are promised, but only when practised by an expert. This is the method by which yogis learn to lie upon thorns, float in water, read thought, "master the elements," and so on.

But we really need not be concerned about these matters. It

is enough that Yoga has made an art, if not a science, of meditation and has opened new paths for us. Aside from self-control and a sense of divine presence, Yoga with its insistence on abstemiousness and freedom from passion does change the whole quality of the personality which comes under its control. The truly meditative man is supposed to have a calm and pleasant voice, poise, tranquility, joy, serenity. I have seen such men in India, where saints are honored above prize fighters, tycoons and movie stars, and I know that they are prodigies of the spirit. The culture that produced them has something to teach us.

Another thing we could learn from India is not to insist upon our own provincial notions of God. Hindus are generally hospitable to all religious—and this must be said even in the face of their occasional hostility (social rather than religious) to Muslims and Christians. The prodigious supply of gods and godly manifestations in India is not a sign of polytheism but of a thirst to find the true God everywhere, in every shape and manifestation and possibility. But Hindu thought is agreed that God is one, and that Buddha and Jesus are among the greatest manifestations of the divine. Are we as hospitable to Buddhist or Hindu insights?

True meditation absorbs all the tribal, local names of the divine into one truth, and welcomes all manifestations no matter from what country or era. Meditation will not get far until it can overcome the parochial, the provincial, the racial. No exclusion clauses can apply to the Absolute.

9

BUDDHIST MEDITATION

OF all the men born into the world, Buddha and Jesus have made the greatest impression upon mankind. Kings and conquerors have altered the borders of empire. Explorers have penetrated every sea and continent from the equator to the poles. Poets and musicians have given expression, sometimes almost unbearably poignant, to that mysterious sense of the beautiful which lies within every human being. Philosophers and scientists have altered our ideas about the nature of reality and of the mind itself. But none of these have had the same impact upon human minds and history as the carpenter's son from Galilee and the king's (or chieftain's) son from Gorakhpur in India.

This in itself is a tribute to men's hankering after truth—that no matter how they stray from it, no matter how they corrupt the original teaching of the founders, they do try to preserve it.

Buddhism was founded upon meditation, and for 2,500 years Buddhists have been practising meditation and developing its techniques. Long, long before the birth of Jesus, Buddhists had learned self-mastery through thought control.

Indeed the whole basis of Buddha's teaching is this from the *Dharmapada:*

"All that we are is the result of what we have thought: it is founded on our thoughts, it is made up of our thoughts."

"Purity and impurity belong to oneself; no one can purify another."

Meditation: The Inward Art

"Be ye lamps unto yourselves. Be ye refuges to yourselves. Hold fast to the Dharma [law or teaching or truth] as a lamp. Hold fast to the Dharma as a refuge. Look not for refuge to anyone beside yourselves."

The truth, as Buddha had discovered it after six years of severe asceticism, is within. The essence of his teaching was renunciation. But this renunciation, though it achieved victory over the usual slavery to pleasure and pain, was not cloistered. It led to self-purification through intellectual and ethical enlightenment, to the love of all sentient beings, and to a life of service.

The Buddha taught that man held his own salvation within his own hands. It was a thing he could work out for himself. Buddhism as Buddha taught it was self-discipline based upon rationality, with an accent upon simplicity and sincerity of life. It was not, as Westerners often think, a philosophy of despair and nihilism, but rather one of cheerful service to others, love of all life, and restraint of irrational desires. But the enlightenment it promised to the faithful followers of the path was intellectual and spiritual. And it was to be attained through plain living and high thinking.

The *Dasa-bhumika Sutra* says, "When thou dost realize that there is no personality in thy mind then thou wilt recognize that there is no reality in things as well." Much of Buddhist thought is subtle. Yet its basis is always practical, based upon experience—which is why it has so fresh an appeal and so hopeful a meaning for us today.

Huston Smith in *The Religions of Man* detects seven important aspects in Buddhism. 1. It was empirical—it appealed directly to personal experience as the final test of truth. 2. It was scientific—basing its judgments upon experience, and on cause and effect, as in the impact of inordinate desire upon human behavior. 3. It was pragmatic—directed toward problem-solving. 4. It was therapeutic—it aimed to overcome suffering. 5. It was psychological, not metaphysical; it dealt practically with human problems. 6. It was democratic, ignoring caste and accepting all. 7. It valued the individual; it taught each individual to rely upon himself and to seek his own salvation in terms acceptable or answerable to his own experience.

Buddha taught that life is suffering, that suffering comes from our cravings, that to overcome craving is to be free, and that this is accomplished by the eightfold path of right knowledge, aspiration, speech, behavior, livelihood, effort, mindfulness, and absorption. Nirvana—a state of bliss in which truth, peace, goodness and supreme reality have been achieved—is the Buddhist goal. An abstemious life, and one of service, is a prerequisite. But the final attainment comes through the arts of meditation, for it is by meditation that one overcomes the five hindrances of sensuality, malevolence, sloth, pride, and a doubting disposition.

Each virtue has, in fact, two vices, two extremes. So we overcome both cruelty and self-pity through compassion, both revenge and lust through love. And meditation is the means by which we realize and grapple with these human failings.

"STOPPING AND REALIZING"

What are the principles of *dhyana,* Buddhist meditation?

Since there are more than ten thousand Buddhist scriptures, many of them dealing with meditation, it is impossible to do more than look at the basic principles and at a few specific methods. But even these are rich in possibility.

"Dhyana," says the Grand Master Chih-chi (sixth century) of Tien-tai, "is the practice of mind-control by which we stop all thinking and seek to realize Truth in its essence." [1]

"Stopping and realizing" is the essence of Buddhist, perhaps of all meditation. "Stopping is an entrance into the wonderful

---

[1] A very helpful anthology of Buddhist scriptures is Dwight Goddard's *A Buddhist Bible,* New York, 1952.

silence and peacefulness of potentiality, while realizing is an entrance into the riches of intuition and transcendental intelligence."

But before we can even begin to meditate, we must follow a few rules—simple, but hard to achieve. We must eat and drink moderately. We must overcome laziness and wasting time in idleness or too much sleep. Before beginning meditation, we must see that the body is tranquil—neither overtired from exertion nor torpid from inactivity.

When we are ready to meditate, we should retire to some quiet place either indoors or out, seat ourselves cross-legged, loosen any tight or restrictive clothing, sway back and forth until we are comfortably balanced, and sit erect so that the nose is in a perpendicular line with the navel. Opening the mouth, we empty the lungs, but slowly so as not to quicken the circulation. Then we breathe with normal quietness, imagining if we like that every pore is also breathing. With eyes closed, we quiet the mind. There are more complicated ways of entering into meditation, but this is the essence.

Now we are ready for meditation itself. Buddhists say that successful meditation requires five mental states—a wishful purpose, a zestful spirit, mindfulness, keen insight and clearness. Wishful purpose means a strong will to practise meditation and achieve its benefits. A zestful spirit means persevering earnestly until the goal is reached. Mindfulness stresses an awareness of the deceptive nature of the world with its fraud and suffering and a sense of what meditation can accomplish. Insight helps us to contrast the benefits of meditation as against the false delights of the world. Clearness about the pain-producing nature of the world will lead us to a singleness of purpose in our practice of meditation as the pathway to bliss. If we are clear about the goal, we shall not be discouraged by one failure or by many, but will persist.

Once meditation has begun, the mind is almost sure to wander

—at least until one has become a master through years of practice. One way of calling it back is to focus attention on the tip of the nose, the space between the eyes, or the navel. Contemplating the navel has become a stock way of joking about Buddhism. But in a hot country where a loin cloth is clothing enough, it is as easy to look at the navel as at the tip of the nose—and for most people a lot easier! Another way is to hold one thought in the mind, or to concentrate on the true nature of all objects of thought. To the Buddhist this means that since every object of thought arises from some cause or condition, it has no nature or being of its own.

We may also control vagrant thoughts by the technique of stopping and examining. If a bad thought enters our minds, we can combat it with a good one. Or we can reflect upon the transitory and therefore insubstantial nature of the thought. Thought itself—even the sense of our own existence—is unreal because it is transient. We can remind ourselves that what we hear or see or smell is only appearance. Therefore we should not be distracted by what our senses report. And when we reflect further that our senses are but part of a body which will die, we lose confidence in selfhood and gain a peaceful and quiet mind.

Buddhists recommend, in fact, that we call up a vision of bodies lying dead and swollen and decaying, as a means of arousing sadness and compassion. If we think about the death and dissolution of the body that most concerns us—our own—and realize that we must submit to the indignity either of being burned to ash or of being slowly eaten and decomposed underground, then surely we must lose all pride and confidence in our own importance. This, Buddhist teachers say, will produce a peaceful and quiet mind.

Next, we should meditate upon the good qualities of our friends, our family, and of those great men and women of the past who have given us the precious heritage of religion, literature and art. We should think also of the good qualities of our enemies, and of animals and all sentient beings.

"When we rise from the practice of Dhyana after these experiences," Master Chih-chi promises, "our hearts will be full of joy and happiness and we will greet whoever we meet with kind and peaceful faces."

The next step is to meditate upon the idea that since all things arise from antecedent causes and conditions, phenomena have no reality, ego has no reality, and we can therefore concentrate our thoughts more peacefully and securely. This idea is strange to the West, but it lies at the center of Buddhist thought, so if we want to achieve the tranquility of Buddhist meditation, we must try to understand it.

The reasoning goes like this. Only that which is permanent and unchanging is real. Everything else is unreal, is appearance, is illusion. Everything in the world we know depends for its existence or functioning upon some antecedent. This means that it has no reality within itself—it is just the outgrowth of something else. Hence it has no complete and true self-ness.

Similarly, everything exists in time. Past flows into present, present into future, and this very flux means that one thing is dependent upon another and therefore not unique of itself and therefore not real. We are so used to thinking of cause and effect, of time and change as proof of reality, that it takes some effort to see the Buddhist view. But when you do see it, you look upon the world as upon a familiar valley seen for the first time from the top of a mountain. So that is how things really are! The school so near the station! It was only having to cross the tracks that made them seem far apart. The cluster of churches, their spires piercing the green shroud of trees, to point like pencils at the sky. The town, so casually swallowed and flattened and overcome by the calm, indifferent countryside.

The Buddhist view of life is something like that. It makes man smaller, but ends by making him bigger. For it sees man born helpless and doomed to death from the moment of his birth. But

128

it surmounts this doom by recognizing it. Only in the mind of man can the unreality of the real be realized and therefore overcome. Admit that this world of appearance is unreal, and you conquer it. There is no other way to win a victory over the otherwise unbearable weight of cause and effect, death and corruption, desire and dissatisfaction, matter and conflict, which crush us. Think about that.

To gain this insight into the transiency of all human experience is a necessary step in Buddhist meditation.

Only mind is real. Mind is eternal, thought transient. Personality—ego—is as much an illusion as material things.

Next, we think about all sentient life and make ourselves conscious of our relationship to it. Not only to man, but also to animals we are bound in a tie of inescapable fraternity.

Finally there comes flooding in to the tranquil mind a sense of the merits of holy men. This phase may begin with a recollection of Jesus and the children, or of Buddha under the Bo tree, or of a saint we have known in our own lives.

Buddhists, like religious-minded people in all cultures who place their emphasis upon meditation, are practical-minded. They rely upon experience. They are suspicious of dogma and doctrine. (I am speaking now of the original Buddhists, and of those who still follow Buddha's teaching instead of the corruptions of it.) They are interested in psychology rather than in metaphysics, in results rather than theories.

One evidence of this is their interest in the mind's control over the body.

"As sickness rises from wrong conditions or maladjustments of good conditions," says Chih-chi, "the followers of Buddha, by observing the Precepts, following the Noble Path and practising Dhyana, should be largely if not wholly free from sickness. Wise control of the mind is the best preventive of sickness and is the best method of cure."

Stop letting the mind dwell upon symptoms, the Buddhists tell us. Make it reflect upon the unreality of the body and of ideas about its condition, and the symptoms will disappear. Most sickness comes from irritations within the mind. Control them, keep the mind tranquil, and you will be well.

Sound advice! The Buddhists were talking and writing this way two thousands years and more before Mary Baker Eddy and Sigmund Freud.

If meditation went no further than this, it would be worthwhile in practical terms alone. But it does go further. By the practice of "stopping and realizing," and the application of this road to enlightenment in all the ways mentioned, one achieves the Supreme Perfect Enlightenment—the common goal of intuition and intelligence, of love and wisdom.

SOME TECHNIQUES

From the incredibly rich literature of Buddhist meditation it is possible to choose only a few of the meditative practices which appear most helpful. Any one of these will no doubt suggest variations.

1. Breathing. Perceive the whole body while you breathe in; perceive the whole body as you breathe out. Calming the body I breathe in, then out. Concentrating the thoughts, breathe in and out. And so on—calming the mind in harmony with calm breath.

2. *Think:* I must be separated by death from all those I love.

3. *Think:* I shall be the heir of all the actions I perform.

4. What is it in my enemy that I hate? Is it his appearance? His walk? His manner? His speech? Eliminate one by one until you have eliminated all. Or if you find the core of your hatred, discover why this fault exists in him and see whether it is brought out or exacerbated by any action or attitude of yours.

5. To initiate concentration, focus upon one of the ten hypnotic circles. Closing your eyes, imagine before you a circle that is blue, or yellow, or red, or white. Or a circle which represents

earth, water, fire, or air. Or a circle of pure light or of empty space. Keep your attention upon this circle as you associate with it the ideas that seem appropriate. In one of these ideas you will find the matter for your further meditation.

6. Place a lump of earth, a flower, or a bowl of water in such a location that you can look at it while meditating. Think of anything and everything that relates to the object, of its relationship to you as the perceiver, of the nature of the relationships between perceiver, object, mental image of the object and the means by which it is conveyed to the brain. Strive for a realization of the insubstantiality of material substance and the universality of perceiving mind.

7. Try to recall in reverse order the events of the previous hour. When this has been mastered, extend the method to several hours, or a day or longer. The exercise should help to concentrate and channel the mind. It may also be used as a means of locating thoughts, problems, persons, events, fears, hopes, and all sorts of unfinished business which would make profitable material for meditation.

8. Practise emptying yourself of self, or of anything belonging to self. *First:* "I am not anywhere." *Second:* "I am not anything to anybody." *Third:* "It is not mine anywhere." *Fourth:* "Nor is mine anything in any way."

9. Develop friendliness for yourself first, then extend it outward to encompass all. To have friendliness for yourself you must be free of enmity which corrodes; free of disquiet; free of illness. You then wish the same for a friend, for a stranger, for an enemy, regarding all equally and the same with yourself.

10. Sit with head erect, breathe deep and slow, and face each point of the compass in turn, sending out thoughts of benevolence and love to all sentient beings in the east, the south, the west, the north. Be aware of the lands, peoples, species in that quarter of the world which you face. Think of that whole vast quadrant as starting from you and broadening out over the rim of the

131

world. Let your concern flow out to those in need—to the refugee, the hungry, the homeless, the oppressed, the mentally disturbed; to young and old, to the pregnant and the dying. Gather them within the arms of your compassion.

11. An exercise in joy. Strive to achieve joy through an approach of five stages. The first joy is merely sensuous, like that of flesh creeping. Then comes the flash of joy, like lightning. Next, the flood of joy like waves breaking and washing over the beach. Then ecstasy. Then an all-pervading, all-encompassing, overwhelming joy.

12. The Four *jhanas,* or raptures. The first stage is one of concentration upon a single thought by means of probing, investigating and reasoning. (This is what we might call the normal or ratiocinative level of meditation.) Second, the mind is detached from reasoning and held still—upon some point of concentration if desired, such as one of the mystic circles. Third, a state of tranquil serenity is reached. Fourth, the mind becomes exalted and purified, indifferent alike to pleasure and pain.

13. Beyond the *jhanas* rise the four *aruppas,* or spheres, achieved by those who devote their lives to meditation. For the sake of completeness, it may be well to include them here, though the novice should not expect to attain them. First comes the sphere of unbounded space to which the devotee ascends by overcoming sensory reactions. Second, the sphere of infinite intellection in which the devotee has merged his thought with the universal mind. Third, ego-consciousness is eliminated and the thinker is no longer aware of himself as self. Fourth, the devotee reaches the sphere in which perception and nonperception are no longer distinguishable.

10

ZEN

"IF I haven't anything in my mind, what shall I do?" asked a Zen student.

"Throw it out," said his master.

"But if I haven't anything, how can I throw it out?"

"Then carry it out."

There is Zen in a nutshell!

Buddhism has had a revival in the Western world through the postwar interest in Zen. Zen, the word itself, is simply a Japanese version of the Indian word for meditation, *dhyana,* by way of the Chinese *ch'an.*

The classical message defining the nature of Zen is this:

"A special transmission outside the scriptures;
 No dependence upon words and letters;
 Direct pointing at the soul of man;
 Seeking into one's nature and the attainment of Buddhahood." [1]

Hui-neng, Chinese Zen master of the seventh century, said that Zen was seeing into one's own nature, and Zen is forever saying in one way or another that enlightenment comes only from within. "Borrowed plumage never grows." The pure Buddha nature is inherent in all; one must learn the art of drawing it out.

Zen therefore leans heavily on experience. Personal experience, not book knowledge, is the road to enlightenment. And

[1] Everyone who tries to understand Zen is indebted to Daisetz Suzuki, from whom this and many other suggestions have been taken. For the plain reader who lacks time to read all of Suzuki, there is a very handy Doubleday Anchor Book titled *Zen Buddhism.* The quotation is from page 61.

experience must be apprehended as it flows, without the disturbance and distortion resulting from analysis and intellectualizing. The infinite is to be found in the finite. Meaning is to be found in facts, not in generalizations. Zen does not separate itself from eating, drinking, work, sleep. It expects understanding to spring from the common life. It is suspicious of words as limiters rather than as expanders of experience. It looks to the everyday experience—listening to a stream, watching the clouds drift across a mountain, quiet meditation—as the path to the awakened life.

Yet there is danger in this necessary reliance upon the senses. For the senses open the way to understanding and at the same time prevent us from understanding. Water refreshes and gives us life. Yet water may also blind and even drown us. We have grown so used to our senses that we do not use them. "Eyes have they, but they see not; they have ears, but they hear not." We need to see as if for the first time.

The philosopher leans upon reason, the orthodox religious person upon revelation or authority. The Zen way is direct apprehension—grasping at what is, and seeing it in its own nature. Zen tries to avoid the human tendency of creating concepts as a way of understanding reality and then treating the concepts as if they were the things they stand for. Zen tries somehow in the moment of identification with an object to awaken to what makes it unique and different. It strives for that moment of understanding in which subject and object lose their distinction, and essence and appearance are one.

It is obvious by now that Zen objects to dualisms, no matter of what kind, as false. Western minds are so accustomed to dualisms as almost the only way of thinking that it comes hard to us to give them up. Mind and body; black and white; freedom and slavery; communism and capitalism; good and evil; heaven and earth; truth and falsehood. Almost everything we see is perceived in this distortion of opposites.

A moment's reflection will convince us that good and evil are intermixed in all sorts of interesting ways; that white is rarely if ever white but something verging on some other color of a spectrum which is continuously and imperceptibly shading off from one color into another; that communism has become more and more a managerial enterprise while capitalism for its own preservation has teamed up with government controls and devices we would identify as socialistic if we were not so unreasonably afraid of the word—all this because we are imprisoned in our narrow dualistic universe and dare not admit that in fact and in reality socialism, communism, capitalism and totalitarianism are mingled together in various ways in various places but are not to be found pure anywhere, since they are abstractions.

If Zen can do nothing else for us, it can free us of the preposterous blinders which have been fastened onto Western man since Plato, or perhaps since Genesis. For it will have nothing to do with the oversimplification of reality that all dualisms imply. It insists that we keep checking back on direct, living experience which like the spectrum is all colors blended into one.

Zen looks upon dualistic distinctions as human inventions, and rather useless ones at that. Flesh and spirit, finite and infinite, eternal and temporal, material and spiritual—all these are illusory distinctions.

Said Hui-neng: "To take hold of this non-duality of truth is the aim of Zen." And again: "The main point is not to think of things good and bad and thereby to be restricted, but to let the mind move on as it is in itself and perform its inexhaustible functions. This is the way to be in accord with the Mind-essence." [2]

Zen tries to come to grips with reality by doing away with dualisms like man-Nature and subject-object, seeing things in the first clear light of dawning consciousness.

Two Zen monks are speaking.

"To whom are you serving tea?"

"There is one who wants it."

"Why don't you make him serve himself?"

"Fortunately I am here."

[2] *Ibid.*, pp. 73 and 170.

From this rejection of duality, Zen slides into a paradoxical position of asserting that there is no self because this implies not-self.

"In the beginning was the Word, and the Word was with God, and the Word was God." In Zen thought there is a beginningless beginning and a Godhead who is nameless and no-word. Other Zen words for this no-word state are mind of no-mind, the un-conscious conscious, or just "this."

"All is one, one is none, none is all." Perhaps this paradox best of all exposes the Zen approach. Quite a load for our yard-stick civilization to get hold of!

The root of Zen is the Buddhist concept of *sunyata*—nothing-ness or void. These are inadequate words. *Sunyata,* as Daisetz Suzuki defines it, is "what makes the existence of anything pos-sible." (Page 261.) It is not intended as an abstract idea, but rather as a word for the oneness which is both immanent and transcendent. Along with this goes the idea of "suchness" (*ta-hata*), the absolute which cannot be understood by means of form. Suchness—which sounds rather ridiculous in English, though there seems to be no better word for it—is also described as the unconscious, a state in which there is neither good nor bad, length nor breadth, time nor eternity.

On the personal level, Zen counsels a habit of mind—or rather no-mind—which is not possessive or grasping. "Take no thought for the morrow." As the monk who has taken a vow of poverty is not cumbered with possessions, so the Zen convert should not be cumbered by his worries, hopes, sorrows—or even by his joys. To this extent the individual puts himself in step with the uni-versal unconscious.

In Buddhist thought all minds are one mind. But mind means no-mind-ness! That is, there is a stage beyond or above con-scious thought which embraces both thinking and not-thinking, a condition prior to separation of mind and world.

This is not the place to explain Zen psychology—there are

many good books which do that. We need only get the feel of it. So we need only to consider one more aspect of Zen thought —its attitude toward nature—before going on to its method of meditation.

ZEN'S VIEW OF NATURE

Zen does not look at nature as antithetical to man. Man is in nature and nature is in man. There is a fundamental identity between them, for nature is that from which we come, in which we live, and to which we return. The goal is therefore to merge into nature and to become one with it—to have those sudden perceptions of oneness with nature which constitute one form of *satori* (enlightenment). Only through such merging does our inner life become complete.

"What is Buddha?" a Zen monk asked a Zen devotee.

"The cat is climbing the post."

"But I do not understand."

"Ask the post."

If you are lucky, this little dialogue will allow you to experience *satori*—a sudden recognition, beyond words, of new meaning, new depth.

Said another Zen master: "A stream of water is flowing out of the mountains, and there are no obstacles that would ever stop its course. The mountain flowers are spread out like gold brocades. . . . The birds in the secluded depths of the woodland are singing their melodies each in their own way. . . . O Monk! What is there that makes you go on reflecting and cogitating?" [3]

The ultimate sense of belongingness is beyond cogitation. It comes in a flash—in that moment when unity is achieved by the merging of conscious and unconscious, "mind and no-mind," observer with object, being with not-being. Zen is very shy about

[3] *Ibid.,* pp. 248, 251.

pinning down this moment, this insight in words, because the experience itself lies beyond words.

Total immersion in the moment, in the act whatever it may be—sleeping, eating, gardening—is one of the things Zen is always recommending. Enlightenment lies within the folds of the here-now.

Zen also tries to combine the biological and psychological man with the social, esthetic, moral, thinking man. It is not anti-rational, but it tries to go beyond rationality by returning the intellectually sophisticated man back to the sources of refreshment which are to be found in his biological, free-wheeling, child nature. It is an innocence reached through wisdom, an awareness achieved through a catlike relaxation which is able at a moment to spring and capture.

SATORI

This much had to be said so that we might understand Zen meditation. Zen teaches a way of meditation which is no meditation at all, but rather a moment of insight—*satori*.

Mahayana Buddhism has two ways of seeking enlightenment. One is intellectual, the other the practical method which leads to a direct, immediate enlightenment. This is what Zen attempts.

But it is not so easy as it sounds. This direct way often leads through years of meditation and years of failure before enlightenment comes.

The method Zen uses is that of the *koan,* or question, which will (eventually) lead the meditator to that moment of recognition which cannot be counterfeited and cannot be mistaken once it comes. Here are some characteristic *koan:*

All things return to the One, but where does this One return?

When you do not think good or not-good, what is your true self?

What are your original features which you have even prior to your birth?

When you seek the Buddha, you cannot see him. The musk-melon is sweet even to the stems, the bitter gourd is bitter even to the roots.

When a monk asked the master to play him a tune on a stringless harp, the master was silent a while, then said, "Do you hear it?" "No." "Why did you not ask louder?"

"If you call this a stick, you affirm; if not, you negate. Beyond affirmation and negation what would you call it?"

What is the sound made by the clapping of one hand?

The intent of the *koan* is to kill the calculating, ratiocinative mind by electric shock, and to free the mind to go beyond the limits of intellection. By this means one comes to recognize the truth that was in his possession from the beginning. It will be something unexpected yet immediately known as right. Then the *koan* will no longer be needed.

The Zen novice is usually counseled not to try to get the meaning of the *koan* from the way it is worded; not to let his imagination seek the answer; not to expect that the *koan* can be captured by considering it as an object of thought; not to seek the answer by logical analysis. Rather, he is expected to use the *koan* as a lever, a vehicle, or a pole. Zen meditation is no meditation!

If other thoughts obtrude, you do not fight them but simply try to get back to the *koan*. Whatever you may be doing, you try to keep it before your mind. At the moment when all appears useless, the moment of realization may be approaching. Sudden intuitive enlightenment occurs only when reason has given up. Then, as Tai-hui says, "something flashes out in your mind, its light will illumine the entire universe, and you will see the spiritual land of the Enlightened Ones."

The Zen master Tosotsu led his students up to three barriers which they had to pass in order to be enlightened. 1. In studying Zen the aim is to see one's own true nature. Where is your true nature? 2. When one realizes his own true nature, he will be free from birth and death. When you shut the light from your eyes and become a corpse, how can you free yourself? 3. If you free yourself from birth and death, your body separates into the four elements. Where are you?

There is fruit for your meditation today, tomorrow, next week!

It should be clear by now that *satori,* the enlightenment that comes from considering a *koan,* is a flash of intuition—a thing that comes only when the bonds of logical thought have been burst and one is ejected into a world of consciousness where truth is felt, seen, apprehended in a self-annihilating moment when seen and seer become one. It cannot really be described; it has to be experienced. As one master put it, "The bottom of a pail is broken through." The mind flows in new channels. The insight somehow merges universal with individual—the goal of all mystics, though Zen is wary of the word.

Satori has to be abrupt, sudden, momentary. It goes beyond language and reason. It overturns habitual ways of thinking. At the moment of recognition, mind and body seem to be annihilated along with the *koan* which led to the enlightenment. Says the Zen master Hakuin: "This is what is known as 'letting go your hold.' As you become awakened from the stupor and regain your breath it is like drinking water and knowing for yourself that it is cold. It will be a joy inexpressible." [4]

This quality—at once irrational yet knowing, commonplace yet transcendental, experience-based yet delving through the experience to a mystery in which all experience is bound, essentially esthetic like the response to a great moment of music—is the quality of Zen.

The word *"satori"* is written in Japanese (and Chinese) with a character which combines heart and mind. So *satori* is something you feel in your own heart. It is not an abstract concept you pick up, like most philosophical ideas, without ever having to experience it. *Satori* therefore should have results affecting all future experience. By bringing self-recognition, it frees one from the chains of illusion, from the false restrictions of formal logic and dualism and ratiocination, and lets one face courageously

[4] *Ibid.,* p. 148.

both life and death, good and evil, existence and nonexistence.

Perhaps the insight of Zen is best conveyed by a Hindu story.

A fish asked its elder: "I have always heard about the sea, but what is it?"

"It is that in which you live and move and have your being. The sea surrounds you as your own being."

TACKLING THE *KOAN*

Now at the risk of raising the ire of Zen masters, I will give you an answer to a *koan* which may help you on your way.

What is the sound made by the clapping of one hand?

Suppose we imagine ourselves to be one of the students filing into the *zendo*—meditation hall—of a Zen temple in Kyoto. We seat ourselves in a room whose light is filtered through hundreds of panes of paper-covered lattice. We compose ourselves in perfect quiet, our hands at rest in our laps, eyes half-closed so that we may look both inward and outward and thus be open to all experience.

As the mind quiets, we bring the *koan* before it again. What is the sound made by the clapping of one hand? We know that *satori* is an experience beyond logical thought and that we are not supposed to solve the problem by logic. Yet we have to begin somewhere. Our hands lie in sight as we look down. Hand, brain and eye together somehow must give up the secret. Why two hands, why ten fingers? What is the logic—the mystery—of ten that makes so neat a basis for all numbers? Could I clap with two fingers instead of two hands?

What is sound? What is silence? What is the condition that is both sound and silence, and neither sound nor silence? The motion of leaves as they turn in the wind before they begin to rustle. Of grain nodding soundless in the field. Of water lapping at the beach in the moment before a wind stirs it to lisp against the pebbles. Of all things that move below the threshold of sound. Ah, the clapping of one hand! *Satori!*

141

Much too simple, no doubt, and much too quickly arrived at, yet perhaps enough to give a hint as to how the mind might work to free itself of logical restraint and ultimately to make the leap across the chasm from habitual thinking to the moment of insight. Take the risk. Make the leap. Feel the abyss beneath you. Feel the strain of muscle yearning for a firm grip on the other side, the bliss of the foot touching firm ground again. In this moment of leaping and landing *satori* must occur. The thrill arises out of the risk. One must leap in order to land.

In *satori* you experience all in a moment the oneness in variety, the universal in the particular, the realization that any particular is an aspect of the universal and inseparable from it in concept and in fact.

Said Ho-yen: "When water is scooped in the hands, the moon is reflected in them. When the flowers are handled, the scent soaks into the robe."

Said Bassui to a dying disciple: "What is the essence of this mind? Your end which is endless is as a snowflake dissolving in the pure air."

A blind man in Japan was offered a lantern when he was about to start home at night.

"I don't need a lantern," he said. "Light or dark is the same to me."

"But someone may run into you."

He took the lantern, but had not gone very far when someone ran into him.

"Watch where you're going," said the blind man. "Can't you see this lantern?"

"Your light is out, brother," came the answer.

HAIKU AS MEDITATION

The best way for a novice to get the feel of Zen and *satori* is through those brief poetic gems of Japan known as *haiku*. A perfect *haiku* embodies a moment of insight which the poet through his art is able to share with the reader. It may be cheating to start with a *haiku* for meditation, since the *haiku* is itself an end-product, the result of a successful meditation. Yet since the chain of art, or of existence, is really endless, it can do no harm to start with one insight and let it lead on, if it will, to another.

Here is a poem of Basho, the greatest of *haiku* writers.

> ON FINDING A DEAD CUCKOO IN THE WOODS
> Hototogisu   (Cuckoo)
> Keshi yuku ho-o ya   (vanishing, go towards)
> Shima hitotsu.   (one island.)

The idea here, of course, is that the world of the living and of the dead are one, that the voice of the living cuckoo and the remembered song are also one. That is the insight—the oneness of life and death suddenly glimpsed, caught, realized, at the moment of seeing that dead cuckoo in the woods.

Translation of *haiku* can easily fall into travesty, the fabric is so delicate. But let us try.

> *O cuckoo—dead*
> *You vanish yet remain,*
> *One-islanded.*

Or:
> *Dead cuckoo bird,*
> *Where, in what island,*
> *Is your voice still heard?*

Or:
> *O vanished bird,*
> *Where is that single island*
> *Where your voice is heard?*

The last comes closest to the Japanese metre of five, seven and five syllables.

Here are a few more, all in translations by Harold Gould Henderson, the most skillful and successful of all those who have tried to catch the delicate, subtle essence of the original.[5]

[5] From *An Introduction to Haiku* by Harold Henderson. Copyright © 1958 by Harold Henderson. Reprinted by permission of Doubleday & Co., Inc.

> *Did it yell*
> *till it became* all *voice?*
> *Cicada-shell!* —Basho

> *Cherry blossoms, more*
> *and more now! Birds have two legs!*
> *Oh, horses have four!* —Onitsura

> *Oh, don't mistreat*
> *the fly! He wrings his hands!*
> *He wrings his feet!* —Issa

In these poems the poet translates himself into the object, sees the world anew, as if for the first time, and fuses himself with the whole of nature which is opened to him by this fresh vision of one small part of it.

Curtis Hidden Page has rendered a very touching poem by Chiyo, a woman writer:

> *I wonder in what fields today*
> *He chases dragon-flies in play,*
> *My little boy—who ran away.*

But the original says merely:

> *Dragonfly-hunter—*
> *Where today*
> *have you gone?*

Which might be rendered:

> *O little boy,*
> *Chaser of dragonflies,*
> *Where now is my joy?*

Here is another, the force of which can be appreciated only by one who has lived through a Japanese winter and then watched the early blossoms unfold one by one:

144

One bloom of plum	(Plum one bloom)
A blossom's worth of	(one bloom's extent of)
warmth—	(warmth)
So let spring come.	—Ransetsu

Then there is Buson's poem, again in Harold Henderson's perfect translation: [6]

> *The scattering bloom—*
> *does it turn into torn wastepaper?*
> *A bamboo broom!*

In each of these, it must be obvious, the poet concentrated on that moment of insight, that thrill of consciousness responding to itself in nature, which is *satori*.

The last of these poems needs a little introduction.

The poet Basho, having lost his way in the fog while traveling in the mountains, inched along a narrow path with the sound of a torrent far below. At last he turned a corner, the fog blew away, and he found himself at the end of a little bridge of vines thrown across a gorge. Henderson renders it this way: [7]

> *Around existence twine*
> *(Oh, bridge that hangs across the gorge!)*
> *ropes of twisted vine.*

This is the finest three-line poem I know in any language. It opens the door to a dozen, a hundred meditations, and I shall not spoil the thrill of self-discovery by saying what they might be. The Zen master might whack us for borrowing our theme instead of being on our own. But like any system, Zen has its limitations too, and we need not be bound by them. In meditation, every man must cut his own path. If these poems afford a new insight or open a path for you, use them. No one has ever done a better job than these Zen-inspired poets, and in so short a space, of merging man with nature, nature with man.

[6] *Ibid.*   [7] *Ibid.*

Once the *haiku* way has been understood—its skill in observation, its ingesting of the experience, and that final outburst which gives new life and meaning to the experience in a flash of poetry —you can start as the poets do with some pulsing of nature which causes your heart to beat faster. Try to catch it in a few words. Never mind whether you are making poetry; just try to catch the experience alive and hold it. Gradually awareness will become a habit, and life will seem fresh at every sip, like cold water from a flowing spring.

GROWING INTO ONENESS

The West in its effort to plumb the meaning of existence fell into the ditch of dualism—a ditch it had first dug itself—and has never really climbed out. The East has floated in a cloud of oneness which often seems to hide both earth and heaven (that dualism again!). Neither view is true. Or both are true, but incomplete. The spectrum—the rainbow—seems to me a better symbol of truth. Life is a continuum, not a page with two sides. Intellect mingles with emotion, emotion with art, art with spirit, spirit with matter again. To respond to the richness of life requires an apparatus that is neither East nor West, emotional nor intellectual, philosophical nor artistic, but all these and more. Meditation is the way of response which overcomes all these false divisions and separations, joining experience and experiencer in one being.

Without this perception of oneness there can be no true meditation. From the East we still have much to learn about ways of growing into oneness. No Eastern insight is more specific, more methodological, and within its framework more successful than Zen.

11

GROUP MEDITATION

HERE and there around the world every Sunday small groups of people come together in unadorned meetinghouses to sit in silent meditation. Such unspectacular meetings have been going on for over three hundred years. A long time to be silent!

The meetings are not always silent, of course. For out of the gathered silence, out of the stimulus to the spirit that comes of meeting together in an expectant silence, messages sometimes come. Or they may not. Some of the deepest Quaker Meetings are entirely silent. And when, at the end, Friends turn to give a firm handclasp to those sitting on either side, there is a warmth of understanding which surpasses words.

Robert Barclay in *The Apology* described the experience nearly three hundred years ago in words that have never been improved upon:

"When I came into the silent assemblies of God's people, I felt a secret power among them, which touched my heart; and as I gave way unto it I found the evil weakening in me and the good raised up; and so I became thus knit and united unto them, hungering more and more after the increase of this power and life."

But why should group meditation be better than private? Barclay again goes to the heart of it when he says:

"As iron sharpeneth iron, the seeing of the faces one of another, when both are inwardly gathered unto the life, giveth occasion for the life secretly to rise, and pass from vessel to vessel. And as many candles lighted, and put in one place, do greatly augment the light, and make it more to shine forth, so when many are gathered together into the same life, there is more of the glory of God, and his power appears, to the refreshment of each individual; for that he partakes not only of the light and life raised in himself, but in all the rest."

If this sounds dubious, Friends would say: Try it. Their only doctrine is the appeal to experience. For them, faith is a thing felt; otherwise it is nothing. Creeds, sacred books, rites, sacraments, liturgies, priesthood, churches and religious institutions are nothing without an inner experience of the presence of the divine. And meditation is the only way one can have it. Wrote George Fox, founder of the Religious Society of Friends, in his *Journal:*

"I saw also that there was an ocean of darkness and death, but an infinite ocean of light and love, which flowed over the ocean of darkness: and in that also I saw the infinite love of God."

This immediate, personal sense of the divine presence within is the basis of the Quaker Meeting, which has no creed, no priesthood, no dogma. George Fox rediscovered the simple truth that God is not kept a prisoner in churches or in books, but that he lives within. "For I saw in that Light and Spirit which was before Scripture was given forth, that all must come to that Spirit—if they would know God or Christ or the Scripture aright—which they that gave them forth were led and taught by." A simple, grand, revolutionary discovery, and the basis of all meditation.

Those who enter a Quaker Meeting for the first time may find it strange. To settle into silence with people all about, sometimes with children squirming and whispering, sometimes with coughing or foot scraping within the room or traffic sounds without, is not easy. When the room quiets at last, the difficulty may increase. What am I supposed to do? What do I fix my thoughts on? How can I be alone with the Alone in all this company?

But gradually you become accustomed to the silence and find yourself merging into it. That all these people have come in order to be silent together somehow guarantees a result, or they wouldn't have gone on doing it for three hundred years. You close your eyes and the silence deepens, as does the sense of merging with the group in a common quest. Suddenly you feel that you are sharing a deep experience, and that this sharing releases you from the prison of individuality, of apartness. In the life of the Meeting you find a new, expanded life. At least, you may. Or if you are not drawn toward contemplation you may not.

"The deepest self of all," says the Quaker writer Howard Brinton, "is that self which we share with all others. This is the one Vine of which we are all branches, the life of God on which our own individual lives are based."

If this is the sort of thing you respond to, you will find fellowship in the stillness, and then a conviction of peace and joy rising to radiant certainty. Silence then is seen to be not empty but very full—a reservoir of memory, a symbol of all that goes before birth and after death—time's symbol, and eternity's. The symbol, too, of holiness: "Be still, and know that I am God."

So Friends gather in that silence without any prearranged program. Each individual should come in a receptive mood, neither prepared to speak nor determined not to speak, but intent upon emptying his mind of everyday matters and getting to the heart of things.

Sometimes the things that come into the mind seem to have a purely personal application. Again, they seem to ask to be shared with others. In this case, one speaks, but with due regard to brevity, reverence, and sensitivity to others. Out of this sharing of both speech and silence comes that strong bond which joins

149

the group together in an active, creative search for divine purpose and meaning.

Sometimes each spoken message grows out of the one before, always with a generous silence between. Here, where each speaker expands and develops the previous message, group meditation is seen at its best, for all minds have centered down on one theme, and the opening given to each individual shapes a corporate discovery of truth. Then it is as if the whole group had joined their minds and spirits together in a union which produced something bigger than any one mind—shared by all, yet leaving to each his own. This is the "gathered meeting," a rare and beautiful experience. (A gathered meeting might also be completely silent.)

First attendance will not be as good as second, nor second as third. Meditation, like learning a language or playing an instrument, takes application. But attendance at Meeting, where there are bound to be men and women skilled in meditation, can be a powerfully strengthening experience to one who seeks to improve his own meditation.

There is, moreover, something uniquely strengthening in joining a group of people who are bound by no preformed creed or doctrine, but are in search of the spiritual truth and guidance that may come to them directly, as it came to the prophets of old and as it has always come to those who put their faith in direct experience rather than in intermediaries—whether priest, institution, ritual or book. The knowledge that they are gathered together for no other purpose, that they have faith in the power of the indwelling spirit thus to express itself, and that their predecessors—not only in the Quaker tradition but in the Hindu and the Buddhist for thousands of years—have proven it experimentally, speaks with freshness and power to any sensitive visitor. And visitors are always welcome at such Meetings, wherever in the world they may be held.

At our Meeting in India at the Quaker International Center in

Delhi there were rarely more than five or six Quakers present. The rest were Hindus, Sikhs, Christians of various sects, Seekers attached to no particular religion, and occasionally a Muslim or a Buddhist. During the difficult months when he was attempting to prevent a break between Hindu and Muslim in independent India, Gandhi used to attend this Meeting, and perhaps for this reason it had kept a special aura of spiritual strength. Yet its strength really lay in the readiness of men of all faiths to gather together in silence, confident that the light would break in upon them and that some of it would emerge in words that would enlarge and strengthen the spirits of all.

Often a Christian, a Hindu and a Sikh would speak to the same opening of truth in a way which would enlarge horizons for everyone. Because there was no ritual or symbolism limiting the group to a predefined notion of completed truth, all were free to speak out of their own experience. It was the variety of religious and cultural backgrounds, and thus the freshness of insights, which gave depth and enlargement to the Meeting. This, it often seemed, is the way religion ought to grow in our time—unconfined, not shut off by creeds as dangerous as international boundaries to the growth of peace and understanding.

Why, I sometimes wondered, is it only from the past that we are willing to accept these rich interminglings of culture and knowledge? It now seems evident that Plato got from the East some of his insights regarding the nature of truth and the spiritual basis of material existence. Christianity took from Neoplatonism the idea of the Word as God—an idea already ancient in India. Buddhism, of course, is a development out of Hinduism. Japanese "Zen" is a corruption of Sanskrit "dhyana"—meditation. Christian communion takes many of its elements from Asiatic mystery cults and they in turn go back to the rites linked with procreation and fertility which are world-wide.

If we look deep enough, all religions are in fact one, and all are authentic. How much bloodshed would have been spared if men had been willing to see this! But religious symbols because of their emotional force have always provided easy reins with which the power-hungry could lead a whole culture or nation into war. And now, ironically, in our own time when religious symbols have grown anemic, we have found ways to heap emotional freight upon secular symbols such as nation, state, and property (private or socialized, either will do) and make them the battle cry and the goad. And the greater irony is this—that the simple act of meditation honestly engaged in could change it all. For no human spirit seeking to be at one with the creative spirit could deny the invitation to be at one with all mankind as the way to be at one with God; nor could he come out of pure meditation without knowing that war is an evil no excuses can justify.

Only how can you make people thirst after pure meditation? It would rob them of their hatreds, their excuses for aggression, their pretense that evil is in the enemy instead of in the self. In our times, perhaps in most times, the idea of the brotherhood of man and the fatherhood of God if totally adhered to becomes treason.

TWO UNIVERSAL LANGUAGES

One reason why the Meeting at Delhi succeeded is that silence is a universal language. When twenty or thirty people sit down in a room and grow silent because they are intent upon the search for truth and significance and spiritual grace, the silence joins them in somewhat the same way as sharing a meal would, or living in a common room, though without introducing the physical problems of either. It lays a hand on them, warm, restraining and encouraging all at the same time—like that of a mother helping her child to walk. It joins them as words read or music sung rarely can do.

For silence is perhaps the greatest symbol of all: the symbol of eternity, of the silence that was before birth and will be after death, of the mystery of space and time and of the stars beyond and the atoms within, of the silent, secret places of the body and the brain, of holiness and deity, of the All which encircles us, of the ineffableness of experience at its ripest, of the sure conviction of divinity that lies beyond expression and that comes to us on rare occasions like an unheard beating of wings seen through a window.

Like silence, deeds of love are also a universal language. If you find a job for a refugee, or feed the dispossessed, or set up an internationally recruited work camp to repair war damage, it does not matter if the servers and the served do not speak the same language. They speak the same silence. The communication between them is often deep and unforgettable.

Friends believe that these two universal languages, of silence and of love, belong together. Therefore out of the silent Meeting has come the ministry of service to the dispossessed. In the silence members come to see that faith and works are really inseparable. If there is that of God in every man—and this one axiom constitutes the whole theology of original Quakerism— there can be no differentiating between man and man or between this man's concept of God and that one's. To serve another is to serve the God in him that is also in oneself; so the distinction of mine and thine is really meaningless. Mary and Martha were both intent upon things that were needful. Work and worship, service and silence belong together; they too are sisters.

Friends, through their work camps, international seminars, and refugee services are simply living out their belief that work is a form of worship. Every Quaker activity begins with a period of silence, and often ends the same way. Friends have no sacraments because they believe all life should be a sacrament of service to the divine that is within. They would agree with Brother Lawrence that the practice of the presence of God is something every moment can participate in, whether gardening or eating or cleaning up or traveling or exercising or meditating.

The Quaker Meeting for Business, usually held once a month, is a practical demonstration of the faith in oneness. There is no *Robert's Rules of Order*. There are no motions, seconds, votes, or decisions by the majority. The Meeting begins in silence. The Clerk introduces items of business. Full and free discussion follows. If disagreements seem to be growing, the Meeting will seek unity in silence. If disagreement continues, the matter will be laid aside for a later Meeting. If the group seems to have reached agreement, the Clerk will read a minute. Changes may be suggested and the minute read again. Finally, if Friends say, "I agree," or "That meets my concern," or something of the sort, and no dissenting voice is raised, the Clerk will declare it to be the sense of the Meeting.

Harmony is confidently looked for and assumed to be present. The usual means of conducting a meeting assumes discord and dramatizes it. What would happen if the parliaments of the world should adopt the Quaker way of doing business? How useful, if instead of the angry debates which have debased the United Nations, there could have been a withdrawal into dignified and probing silence while members, moved by the uniting divinity they share, could have searched for it within themselves and brought it out in a suggestion all could accept.

Friends Meeting is based on a faith in that deeper unity which underlies all discords, all conflict. The search for unity when confronted with a debatable issue is not compromise, but rather a deeper understanding of the differences, leading to a deeper unity and a satisfactory solution. Our strange fear of bargaining and compromise in the political arena might be overcome if we could learn to use the Quaker way, not of fighting every inch of the way to a compromise satisfactory to no one, but of seeking unity in a solution which responds to all legitimate needs and interests.

WHAT LOVE WILL DO

It naturally follows from the Quaker axiom of the uniting presence of the divine in every individual that all are equal (hence no discrimination or prejudice) and capable of conducting their own affairs through voluntary association in various social, religious, professional, cultural or political groups, that peace is a way of life which can be achieved through the proper application of faith and works, and that simplicity is to be encouraged in all things—dress, manner of life, speech. Quakers brought Germans, French, Dutch and Swedes as well as Quakers from the British Isles into their holy experiment in Pennsylvania, as Penn himself noted in 1685. Under the umbrella of Quaker permissiveness and respect, all these cultures were free to go their own way, and eventually to flow into the American mainstream.

Western civilization, trapped in the dualisms from which it rarely escapes, has been arguing over means and ends. Are any means justified to bring about a desirable end? By adopting unworthy means, do we alter our ends in the very process of pursuing them?

Quaker thought would point to motive as the key to this door. It is the motive in our acts which determines our choice of means. As William Penn wrote in that little book, *Some Fruits of Solitude,* which Robert Louis Stevenson discovered with such delight two hundred years after it was written:

"A good end cannot sanctify evil means; nor must we ever do evil, that good may come of it. . . . Let us then try what Love will do: for if men did once see we love them, we should soon find they would not harm us. Force may subdue, but Love gains; and he that forgives first, wins the laurel."

This simple statement puts ends and means in their proper perspective: works emerge from a worship of the divine within, issuing in love. With this motive, Penn urges, conflicts could be

155

resolved. He proved it in Pennsylvania where Quakers and Indians lived at peace. Ironically, nuclear warfare has now proven Penn's way to be the only alternative to annihilation.

Historically, Quakers belong to the stage of religious development called Quietism, which develops at some point in every faith. Then ritual is abandoned and the devotee grows confident and serene in his direct experience of contact with the divine. Its ethic is one of nonviolence. It does not judge others but counsels forgiveness and love. The Beatitudes offer the world's most perfect expression of Quietism. The Bhagavad-Gita, despite its curious advice to Arjuna to carry on the war, is otherwise in the same vein, as are many other Hindu and Buddhist scriptures.

In Christian history the term Quietist (hesychastae) was first applied to those living in separate cells of a religious community, then to the monks of Mount Athos in Greece who, beginning in the fourteenth century, began to speak of a divine light. This same light has guided many a Christian mystic since. Emerson called it the Oversoul. "The highest revelation," he wrote, "is that God is in every man." When asked about his religious position, he said: "I am more of a Quaker than anything else. I believe in the 'still small voice' and that voice is Christ within us."

The confident faith that the divine may be reached not through intellect or senses but by the indwelling spirit which is itself divine unites Quakers to men of many faiths in various times and places. It could unite us today.

GROUP SILENCE

Well, then, what do you *do* in a Quaker Meeting?

First, you simply settle yourself physically so that you will be comfortable without having to move and shift about.

Then you listen to the silence, testing its depths, lights and shadows. Awareness of the fertility of silence may itself lead to fruitful meditation, or to meaningful memories. Silence keeps

green the memory of those we have lost and joins them with the divine. Or by painfully reminding us of our shortcomings, it prods us to do better.

The silence will make us aware of those who sit with us, and by searching inwardly we may come to know them better. Or we may feel them not as individuals but as a group of which we are a part—which we belong to and merge with. Then suddenly we feel their presence almost physically as a strength which enters into us and becomes our strength. We are joined together in one body and in one search.

Next, we might rest upon this ocean of strength as an oarsman, letting the current carry us where it will. Our waiting may be rewarded by a flash of insight or memory or joy. We can then let ourselves be borne upon that current. A beloved teacher, an Indian Quaker, has told me that when his thoughts are joyful he does not permit them to continue too long since this might run into self-indulgence. Nor does he let unhappy thoughts disappear as they tend to, but holds them and examines them to make sure that they are not hiding some self-truth he has been avoiding.

But waiting in silence may turn into aimless daydreaming or idle vacuity. In that case, one must rouse himself to deal with a problem—personal or public—that has been concerning him. The embracing silence of the group often helps both by support and stimulus to lead one through to an insight or a solution that would otherwise not have been grasped.

The Meeting also gives us a wonderful opportunity to search our experience for what we can honestly believe. Since any intellectual growth results in a change and deepening of belief, personal religion is always changing. By sharpening our faculties of observation, by being sensitive to people, to nature, to books, to ideas, to arts we deepen our experience. Meeting offers a time, unlikely to be found elsewhere, when we can consolidate these gains, see them in perspective, shape them to an ever more perfect form. If we are engaged in such a creative act, things said in Meeting often open new insights and seem to provide exactly what we were seeking.

If none of these gets results, we may direct our thoughts to some remembered person or scene or event, to a poem or piece of music or painting, to some loved verse from Bible or treasured book, and meditate upon that.

But intellectual meditation is not the final goal in Meeting. The goal is a sense of vital, freshening oneness with the divine. We move from the creation to the creator, from the natural to the supernal, from the lone individual to the individual merged in this group and then in all mankind, from the individual self to the wider self that embraces all existence, all the past, all potentiality; from the divine within to the divine All.

Out of this enlargement comes a sense of freedom, of love towards all. The little self now seems a merely incidental thing. The larger self has scooped up all matter, all spirit and become one with it. The well of living water flows pure and clear. The light shines that is a light unto our feet and a lantern unto our paths. We are healed, uplifted, freed.

"Deep calleth unto deep at the noise of thy waterspouts; all thy waves and thy billows are gone over me." (Psalms 42:7.)

The oarsman no longer relies upon the frail boat which preserves his weak self from the waters. He has dived into the deep and become one with it. Its strength rises under him and makes him float. The waters cleanse him; the waves force him to go with the current. "All thy waves and thy billows are gone over me." The little self has merged itself into the greater strength. The Meeting has become, as it was intended to be, a meeting of the human and the divine.

12

QUAKER MEETING

I have seated myself in Meeting, quieted my body and so far as possible left it to itself and grown unaware of it. I have swept away the trifles that clutter the floor of my mind, and put the room in order. I have sent my thoughts toward one member of the group whom I do not know particularly well and whom I want to know better, and I have tried to see into his particular qualities, interests and needs, and how we might become more meaningful to each other.

I have taken down a problem from the shelf and tried to look at it without fear or prejudice. It may be a personal problem, such as the fault of flaring up over trifles or being too rigid about my work schedule when human needs push in. I may try to look at it as if it belonged to someone else—it's always so much easier to locate someone else's fault and see the solution! I might even pretend that the problem belongs to a particular friend or family member and then see how I would counsel him out of it.

Or it may be a community or world problem. Our world affords ample material for serious meditation!

But this is not the level I want to stay at. I seek a deeper one. I may find my way into it by recalling a person, now dead, who has become a part of me—a teacher, an aunt, a poet. Or by way of some dearly remembered scene or incident of childhood, or of a beloved place. Through my sense of oneness with something outside myself I am seeking oneness with all.

It may be that a line or two of poetry or a verse of the Bible will come into my mind.

"Be not conformed to this world; but be ye transformed by the renewing of your mind."

"The Lord is my shepherd; I shall not want."

"Blessed are the peacemakers: for they shall be called the children of God."

Any one of these may open the gates into that deeper awareness of the life we share with the past, with beauty which becomes ours as we drink it in, with creativity.

I have not come to Meeting with the idea of speaking. Nor have I come with the idea that I will not speak. I have come in order to enter into that deeper life, to feel myself part of that stronger current. If as I go with that current I feel filled with a message that ought to be shared, I will try to share it. Many of the thoughts that come in Meeting are for myself alone, and usually I can recognize them. But if words detach themselves from a purely personal experience in such a way as to suggest a shape and substance that is communicable, I will speak.

It is not easy to speak in Meeting, especially the first time. It may grow easier with experience, but it never goes to the point where one can feel that he has really said all that he had intended, or that he had fully delivered the message or the vision that seemed so clear before he began to speak. Speaking in Meeting is therefore like painting or writing or composing. It is in the realm of art. The vision is perfect but the rendering is full of flaws. Right here in the act of giving voice to vision, of meditating and then delivering the goods, we sense that imperfect union of the human and the divine. The voice within speaks authentically. Yet when as human vessels we try to pour it out, something is lost. So the act of meditation itself underscores both the union and its weakness on the human side.

It is not considered fair play to come to Meeting with a talk already prepared, though I suspect it has been done. It is felt to be a good idea to prepare the mind beforehand, however, by reading a chapter from the Bible or from some other religious work, or anything else which may have deepening qualities.

Sometimes I do read something of that sort on a Sunday morning, but more likely—since a good deal of reading is part of my working life—I will find when I get to Meeting that some text which has impressed or puzzled me during the past week will arise and repeat itself. It may turn out to be something I would like to share with my friends.

A message may be as brief as one sentence. Many will remember the humor and sweetness of the scene in the film, "Friendly Persuasion," where the little boy delivered himself in Meeting of the message: "God is love."

I might feel moved to say something as simple as this, as I believe I did once:

"We keep putting off the day when we shall have time to be happy, when we shall have time for the important things, when we can have our work done and all our little duties attended to. Then, we promise ourselves, we shall really live. But so long as we go on telling ourselves that we shall do it tomorrow, we are really seeing to it that there shall be no such tomorrow. And in truth, there may not be. Let us do it now."

Not very profound. Granted. But it may just happen to speak to the condition of someone in the group. It might even change a life. That is the adventure inherent in every Meeting.

No one expects fine oratory or a polished essay in Meeting. Words too perfectly uttered would be suspect. Earnestness, sincerity, and a warmness as from the heart are the things looked for. What I listen for are words, as George Fox said, which speak to my condition.

But sometimes the fruit of meditation in Meeting issues in a more fully developed idea or insight. I place several of these here, as well as I can remember them. In no case did I suspect their imminence when I went to Meeting. It was as a result of

Meeting—its silence, the presence of others, the emergence of thoughts and feelings submerged in the mind but raised by the buoyancy of the Meeting itself, which brought them into being.

A MEDITATION ON THE DIVINE LIGHT

"And God said, Let there be light: and there was light."

This wonderful guess about the start of the world may not be far wrong, according to the latest scientific ideas. It also suggests the necessity of concept before creation, of thought before act. There is an implication too that for the divine creator (and however we may conceive the creative force, our presence in a perceivable world makes the creation an axiom), conception and creation flow easily from one to the other. But for us, the gap between is perilous. We find it a good deal easier to think of doing something than to do it. We have good intentions which somehow never grow into action.

We can imagine, since brain waves and light and matter are all known to involve electrical impulses, that somehow to the creator (or creative force if you prefer) conception and creation are impulses in a continuous spectrum. One flows easily into the other. So we might imagine that if we knew how to tune in on the divine light of creation, we might discover this continuous wavelength. Then our acts too would flow naturally from our thoughts. Thinking a good thing and doing it would be as one. Instead, we are all the time thinking of the good things we would like to do and are quite capable of doing, and then not doing them. Between the thought and the act gapes the wide chasm of indifference or laziness.

Could we by continuous practice learn to make our thoughts and acts one harmonious vibration? Then we would be true to the divine light that shines within when we let it; that shone in the very creation of a world which is our heritage since in some obscure but certain fashion our being was implicit in its beginning. Then, as we became more and more the creator merging thought and act, we would sense our privilege and our power as a part of that light that was in the beginning.

A MEDITATION ON FAITH AND SCIENCE

> *Faith is a fine invention*
> *For gentlemen who see;*
> *But microscopes are prudent*
> *In an emergency!*
>
> —Emily Dickinson

Do we have to chose between faith and microscopes? Emily Dickinson in her poetry keeps showing us that paradoxical quality that is in all mystics—the combination of a literal, scientific matter-of-factness, power of observation and rootedness in experience teamed with a power to soar straight up in sudden ecstasy. She knew how to fuse faith and microscopes. Other Americans have known too.

Walt Whitman who was half a Quaker, Emerson who said he was more a Quaker than anything else, and Whittier who was all Quaker—each in his special way combined the matter-of-fact with the poetic, stars with steel mills, faith with microscopes. Mystics, unlike orthodox believers, are unafraid of new truth. Mysticism is experience. It hungers for any evidence that is concrete, capable of being felt. A poet is a mystic in the realm of art; a mystic a poet in the realm of religion. Either quaffs experience eagerly, ingests it, and then makes poetry or ecstasy of it. There has to be this turning inward.

But David Riesman has been telling us that the mark of modern character is its turning outward, looking to others for guidance rather than to the inner voice or monitor. The symbol of the other-directed, he tells us, is the antennae of the insect, responding to touch rather than to light.

Some of us are old-fashioned; we still look within. But this doesn't mean giving up microscopes. The clearest vision seems to come from a combination of faith and microscopes—from mystic faith and vision plus scientific accuracy and patience.

They are not incompatible. Both the mystic and the scientist work upon experience, often from unproved premises, and with faith in the ability of the human mind to get at the truth. And either religion or science, if it is vital and confident, must be willing to change as evidence accumulates. If Jesus were teaching today, he would not be talking about vineyards but about atomic structure and about men like Sir Alexander Fleming, whose insight, akin to that of the mystic, enabled him to see from an accident to his culture plates that moulds might be used to combat bacteria.

What we see in the microscope will often confirm what we have guessed by faith. What science discovers, faith can work into a wider tapestry. We need both faith and microscopes.

A MEDITATION ON FREEDOM

We are prisoned by our aloneness, but liberated by our belonging to mankind. We are prisoned by our sameness to all men, but liberated by our uniqueness. That both these things are so is a paradox.

We are prisoned by our hatreds and meannesses, but liberated by love. Yet these two things spring from the same fountain, and how shall we separate them? Or how shall we know love from hate, when we are often hardest on those we love best, or are fettered by what we call love in the tightest of prisons?

We are prisoned by our logicality and liberated by our ability to transcend the logical through intuition. Yet at the same time we are prisoned by emotions that will not let us be logical.

The prison and the freedom are inextricably united. Perhaps we could not breathe the air of freedom with gratitude if we did not know the stink of the prison.

164

Life both chains and liberates; death both chains and liberates. There are two sides to the prison bars, but sometimes we cannot tell which side we are on. We look at the animals in the zoo and we see that they are behind bars. But to them do we not appear so? And are we not? And how do we free ourselves?

If we cannot escape from the prison of self, can we ever be free? If we cannot escape from the prison of togetherness, or of sameness, can we ever be free? Is there such a thing as freedom, or is it only an illusion—prisoned as we are in our biological inheritance, in what we have been taught from youth, in the very train of circumstances that makes us who and what and where we are, that determines by these chances much of what happens to us?

Or is freedom only the ability to recognize that we are not free? Or is it the gradual acceptance of all the prisons wherein we are prisoned and the chains wherewith we are chained, and the enlightened knowledge that we must build our freedom within these prisons, and make our captivity an opportunity, and cherish the chains that bind us to something because even being bound is a kind of safety, a kind of security, a kind of freedom?

We cannot escape our emotions, but we can learn to school, to train, and to elevate them. We can hold them within bounds, and in this binding grow freer. So to chain ourselves in part is to free ourselves in substance. There is no freedom without such chains. What freedom we have we gain only by learning how to count our steps within the cage we are born in. And how in fancy to leap over the wall, or in faith to wait for the sure release.

A MEDITATION ON DOUBT

Doubt is equally important with faith in living religiously. In honest doubt we grapple with the problems that really matter, push aside the surface clichés and half truths and tired formulas that strangle most organized religion, and come close to the heart of things. Doubt is like a mountain path leading to the summit. It makes struggle a necessity, but it leads upward. No saint or religious leader has found his way to faith except through doubt. For doubt shows that the seeker is experiencing something within himself, and only through an inner experience which shakes the seeker into new life can faith find firm footing.

High in the Himalayas I visited a camp of Tibetan refugees. After their leader had greeted me by presenting the traditional scarf, he led my wife and me into a rough building which served as a temple. Rows of little butter lamps threw their golden light upon paintings of the Buddha. In a small dark room apart stood a brightly painted sedan chair. As we were led up to it, an aged lama picked up a mirror and focused sunlight on the front window of the chair so that there suddenly sprang to view a white, masklike face. A dead lama, our interpreter whispered. A very holy man, who before his death had foretold that he would come to life again. The refugees, fleeing from the Chinese Communists, had carried him hundreds of miles over the highest mountains in the world.

Later I met the Dalai Lama, an earnest, deeply religious young man who had also had to flee his country. When the previous Dalai Lama died, wise men had gone forth to seek the new holy one, had found a little boy who recognized things that had belonged to his predecessor and could pick them out unerringly from among similar objects. Identified by these and other signs, he had been brought back to Lhasa and enthroned with rejoicing.

So here is a religion where an infant is born obscurely, recognized by wise men and worshiped; where a holy man prophesies that he will return from the dead.

Does this make me suspect Christianity? Good—face the doubt. Virgin birth, infant god, the holy one violently killed, his flesh eaten, yet resurrected—these are repeated themes in the history of world religions. As I let my mind take hold of this fact I come to see that these repetitions do not palliate or cancel the strength of the Christian story. Rather they are reinforcing examples of the universal religious impulse and of the way man seeks to represent the cycle of death and rebirth that runs through all of nature. In Tibetan Buddhism, with its firm faith in the rebirth of the soul not only of Dalai Lamas but of all, and of a progress based upon behavior during past lives, this impulse is dramatically present.

"Lord, I believe; help thou mine unbelief." (Mark 9:24.)

Does this perhaps mean that the road to vital faith is through unbelieving vitally, energetically, questingly, until every doubt has been turned inside out, until every false pretense at belief and every unacceptable assertion about God has been swept away, leaving a faith that is sturdy not like a Gothic cathedral with all its decorations, but like a Greek athlete poised naked to begin the race?

A MEDITATION ON FORGIVENESS AND GUILT

Sometimes in meditation two separate ideas come together in such a way as to suggest a new opening.

While I was living in India, I drove one day past the jail at Karnal. On the gate in boldly sculptured letters stood the words "Hate the sin, not the sinner."

Several days later during Meeting I had begun to ask myself the question, Who am I? Am I the unique individual Rousseau found himself to be? Or an anonymous drone in a colony of ants as the behaviorists once asserted—prisoner of a biological past and a conditioning environment over which I have no control?

The words on the jail came back to me. How did it happen that I sat here in this comfortable room, surrounded by friends, instead of in a cell of that jail? How had the guilt in me escaped jailing?

Within myself I find altogether too much hate, anger, cruelty, meanness. They tie me to those in whom these faults burn hotter and land them in jail, and to the terrible human evils of war, murder, genocide, atrocity. Why, when I read of crimes of violence, of sexual assault, of riots and lynchings, does my blood pressure rise? Is it because deep within I share the urgings and temptations of the criminal?

Oh, it is easy for me to excuse myself my bursts of anger or meanness. This is not the real self, but a momentary aberration —the "temporary insanity" of the courts in miniature. Exactly! So my forgiveness must stretch to all—to those whose aberrations have stretched into crimes.

But have I any right to forgive those who have injured others?

"Father, forgive them; for they know not what they do." "Forgive us our trespasses as we forgive those who trespass against us." Or against any.

Each trespass involves all.

We of the West trespassed upon China for decades. The result is Communist China's trespass upon Tibet—an historical consequence that can be clearly illustrated. Who taught imperialism to Japan? Who practically wiped out a whole race in order to take over their continent, then called the murdered race "savages"?

Each of us is inescapably involved in mankind, in all its sins and triumphs. The conclusion is that we have to assume all these obligations and then try to reconcile with love. Those whom we hate, others may love. So those whom others have injured we must nurse and cherish.

"Love was the first motion," said the Quaker John Woolman, explaining his concern to go out among the Indians. In order to convert them? No, but that "I might receive some instruction from them, or they might in any degree be helped forward by my following the leadings of truth among them."

In that noble humility of John Woolman lies the whole solution to our dealings with each other, whether in family, community, or community of nations. If we all knew how to help others forward by following the leadings of truth in them, there might soon be no jails, no murders, no wars. Unhappily, it is a very large if.

MEDITATION AT A QUAKER WEDDING

[Quaker weddings are very simple affairs. Friends and families of the bride and groom enter the meetinghouse and sit in silence. Bride and groom enter together and sit near the front. When they feel moved to it, they rise and speak their vows to each other. A member of the Meeting then reads the marriage certificate. In the silence before or after, any who feel so moved may speak.]

Marriage is the fulcrum upon which life rests and gets its leverage. Until this time, life is parturition. First there is the separation from the mother's body, then from her breast. Then from the home—first for a few hours at school, then perhaps away to college and a job in some other city. All these partings are necessary to the making of a self-reliant, mature person. And for a while the sense of freedom that comes of these somewhat painful separations dominates the mood of the young adult, giving him or her those qualities of gaiety, self-assurance, confidence and optimism that are so endearing—and to many of us so poignant.

On this fulcrum life balances, swinging free as a child who, standing in the middle of a seesaw, can with a slight shift of weight move the board either way. This period of freedom is as brief as the point of the fulcrum is short in relation to the whole board, the whole life. For no life grows complete by separation. The separations were necessary in order that the reverse trend might set in.

Marriage is the beginning of completion. Now male and female are joined as nature and the divine plan intended. Now a home is to be built, not left. Children will make their appearance to repeat the cycle. From the young pleasures of self-indulgent freedom the couple, reinforced by the counsel they are able to give each other, step forward to the solider pleasures of service to the neighborhood, the church, the community they belong to. Only when the life of the group and its responsibilities have been taken up by the new family can the individual feel complete.

The fulcrum of life which gave them support for a free ride now supplies that firm wedge to push against as they raise the burden they have willingly taken on. It happens that the Latin meaning of *fulcrum* is "bedpost." The bed is our traditional symbol of marriage. So our very language has recognized that marriage is indeed the fulcrum of life.

A MEDITATION ON CHRISTMAS

One of the remarkable things about the Christmas story is how things come in threes. First there is the family—Jesus, Joseph and Mary. Then come the shepherds. The Bible does not tell us how many, but the charming medieval mystery plays usually introduce three, with their gifts, just as there are three wise men with their gifts of gold, frankincense and myrrh.

The gifts, as we all know from the beautiful Christmas carol, have meaning—gold because he shall be "King forever," frankincense which "owns a Deity nigh," myrrh for the bitterness of "sorrowing, sighing, bleeding, dying."

Each gift establishes another trinity—that of the gift, the giver and the taker. So each of the wise men through his gift ties himself to the infant, as each of us comes at Christmas with a gift to tie ourselves to each of those we love. Each of those givings which together make Christmas for us establishes another trinity of exchange like that of the wise men. Though not at all prophetic, we too have tried to pick the right gift—the gift not only suitable for the one we give to, but suitable as coming from us, so that it strengthens the relationship between us.

Because they are related to Jesus, these gifts we make at Christmas have a specially sacred quality. They are symbols of that love which made of Jesus a gift to mankind, thus establishing a link between the human and the divine which remains with us even today. "Unto us a son is given." Not only to Mary, to Joseph, but to us. And not only in this one birth, but with every birth the wings of the divine and the mysterious brush over us. Heaven bends to earth, so close that we hear the angels sing. Here is another trinity—heaven, earth and man. Through the divine in man, most fully revealed in Jesus, heaven and earth draw close, not only at the distant horizon but around the globe.

Perhaps the truth men groped for when they decreed a sacred Trinity was just this. From the creator, the author of life, or the mind comes the gift in which creation is made manifest in the body—the son. The spirit, the spirit of creativity is the divine gift which informs and invigorates all. Mind, body, spirit—the gifts of Christmas bring us back to that.

Gold of the divine reign; myrrh of the bitter bodily death; incense of the mysterious, indwelling, undying spirit. Inseparable trinity of our heritage, part human, part divine, but at Christmastide so intermingled that we can scarcely tell the one from the other. Which is as it should be, since truth is one.

A MEDITATION ON EASTER

In our concentration on the particular drama of Easter we are in danger of overlooking its wider significance. Easter is the festival which relates the living to the dead—so significantly that once its meaning is grasped, life takes on a new dimension.

Except it die, how can it be quickened? In this question, which contains its own answer, lies the whole significance of Easter, and perhaps of all life.

171

Meditation: The Inward Art

The connection between life and death is in the end a mystery, but it is real. Every evidence of nature shows that although particular lives must end, life itself goes on abundantly. Out of decay, out of the great wheel of the seasons new life comes, yet always dependent on the old. The dead plant transmits its seed to the future. Last year's leaves make a compost for this year's garden. The calf becomes a heifer, and being impregnated with living seed in its turn gives birth and then freshens and keeps up the bountiful flow of milk which nourishes our young. Both evolution and the necessity of eating tie us from the beginning of time to the animal and vegetable worlds as well as to the human. The mystery of the living seed ties us to an inheritance beyond recorded history.

This is a tie which binds us both to the past and to the future: by inheritance to the past, by our memories of the dead to a future in death which we cannot envision. But in our memories of the dead we have our surest tie to what lies beyond life for us too. The love which cherishes is the power that keeps the dead among the living. In what sense is Jesus alive today? Is it not clear that his life is in our lives—in our memory of his words, his life, his example, his divinity? What a miracle, that for two thousand years he has lived in millions of hearts and minds—one person, yet divided among millions, and more strengthened the more he is divided? The emperors, the aristocrats, the statesman of his time are forgotten, yet this obscure carpenter's son lives.

So may all of us, in our proportion and to the degree that we try to be like him.

As Jesus lives in us, so do our grandparents, our teachers, our companions of childhood. Living or dead, they are a part of us. So are Shakespeare, Beethoven, Socrates. Our life roots are deep in this rich soil. "Except it die, how can it be quickened?"

Even biologically, when you calculate the number of descendants a man ten generations back can have today, the truth of this mystery grows clear.

But it is in the warmth of a loving memory that the mystery grows clearest.

When my father died, we followed the usual custom in his community of holding visiting hours when friends could take a last look at him. I dreaded it. The custom seemed ghoulish to me, even barbarous. But I determined to be on hand for every minute of it.

It turned out to be an unforgettable and heart-warming experience. His brothers and nieces, exposing an affection we too often fail to reveal directly, told me things I had never known about him. His dearest friend dropped in. I had expected and feared a rather lugubrious sermon. Instead, warm and smiling memories of their early days together. Men I did not know came to tell how he had found them a job, given friendly encouragement, made them feel welcome in church, and had taken them as strangers into his home. I discovered then that my father lived on in many lives, not only in mine and my brother's. In one way or another all of us will pass this along. I am not at all sure, for instance, that I would feel compelled to put time into community affairs or give much thought to religion if it were not for my father's example. And perhaps I shall hand on something of this to my son. And so on, in a demonstrable immortality.

Bach lives every time I bring one of his fugues to life with my feet and fingers. I open a book of Emily Dickinson's poems and she leaps alive from the page. In the marbles of the Parthenon not only the sculptors but the models have life unending. The old house we live in, the pieces of silver or china we use— all remind us of people who live in us.

Easter reminds us not only that Jesus lives but that all life is renewal—an assertion that out of death life keeps coming on and is continually enriched.

173

Meditation: The Inward Art

ANOTHER MEDITATION ON EASTER

In Matthew's beautiful telling of what happened on the first Easter morning, the story of the two Marys meeting the angel at the sepulchre ends with these amazing words: "And they departed quickly from the sepulchre with fear and great joy."

Fear and joy together? How can that be?

As this phrase has been echoing in my mind, I have tried to put it to the test of experience. The first thing that comes to mind is falling in love. The very color of that joy is the fear that the one you love may not feel as you do; that she won't be there when you go to seek her; that you will say something to offend her; that you aren't worthy of her—which of course you aren't—that she will fall in love with someone else; that love like this can't last. Fear and great joy seems to be an almost perfect expression of what it is like to be in love.

Most men, if they remember how they felt when they stood up in church waiting for their bride to come down the aisle, will readily agree that at this memorable moment too they felt that strange mingling of fear and joy.

When the young mother enters into labor she, too, knows how joy and fear are joined. Or when, a few years later, she sends her youngster off to school for the first time and returns to a strangely quiet house. That separation is full of fears, yet marks the joy of knowing that the child has taken a first step toward maturity.

When the child, growing into manhood, goes off to college and no longer is safely under the parental roof each night, this step toward maturity also brings—to the parents at least, and maybe for the boy or girl too—a feeling of fear mingled with joy.

If he makes some sort of success, so that he has to appear as a speaker, or act on a stage, or later on make decisions that will affect many lives beside his own, these moments, too, will combine fear with joy. In fact, this seems to be the very test of our great moments, that they are compounded of fear and joy.

And if this is as true of our high moments as it was for those watchers at the sepulchre, isn't it likely that death, too, will be another such moment? What Easter seems to say to us, therefore, is this: Live your life to the full, savoring those high moments which mingle fear with joy, confident that after life has been lived in that high spirit you, too, like those watchers at the sepulchre, will depart with fear and great joy.

175

13

MYSTICISM

MEDITATION is an open door to a wider life for anyone of normal intelligence. The door is open alike to the religious, to skeptics, to agnostics or atheists, and perhaps the atheist has more need of it than anyone. But meditation, it seems to me, cannot be fully satisfying, it cannot have its finest results, unless we are willing at least to try walking the mystic road. We may not be struck blind with the glory as Paul was on the way to Damascus, but even a lesser illumination may have profound results.

We do not need to be frightened by the words mystic and mysticism. To many they may have a distant, oriental sound. Mystic knowledge may seem beyond the reach of the ordinary person—a something to be experienced only by saints.

But this is not so. The early Christians, simple people, had it. Men and women without formal education have been enriched by it, as well as great religious teachers like Jesus, Ramakrishna and Socrates.

Meditation is a method of filtering experience through the mind so as to give it meaning and direction. Meditation may or may not lead to an intimation of the divine and a sense of oneness with it. It may work very usefully on a problem of ethics, human relations, family tension, self-analysis, or some weighty community or international matter. But to stop there is like using a piano to play only chords when there is all of Chopin, Beethoven or Bach waiting to come out of it. Meditation is not complete unless it works its way upward to the mystic union of one with All, of soul with Soul.

It is strange that the word "mystic" suggests something distant and unknowable to many, when the whole point of mysticism is to come close to the divine, to experience it fully, deeply, personally. It is "an immediate inward revelation of God within the sphere of personal experience." [1] The true mystics are concerned more with practice than with theory; it is the living experience of the divine presence, the union of the self with the All that they seek.

Says the Quaker writer, Rufus Jones, in *The Trail of Life in the Middle Years:* "The essential characteristic of it is the attainment of a personal conviction by an individual that the human spirit and the divine Spirit have met, have found each other, and are in mutual and reciprocal correspondence as spirit with Spirit."

And again, in *Studies in Mystical Religion:* "Mysticism is the type of religion which puts the emphasis on immediate awareness of relation with God, on direct and intimate consciousness of the Divine presence. It is religion in its most acute, intense and living stage." He never tired of emphasizing the power of mystical insight to sweeten and strengthen the daily life. "The spirit of man is the candle of the Lord." (Proverbs 20:27.)

Mysticism is the universal religion. It is the main root of Hinduism, as we have seen. In China, Taoism saw the whole universe as a vital organism. The individual and the cosmos are related to each other in such a way that man by his very nature is involved in all cosmic events. The prayer of Kwan-yin-tze beautifully expresses this mystic universalism:

"Let my essence be merged in the Essence of heaven and earth and all things, as different waters could be combined in one water. . . . Let my spirit be merged in the Spirit of heaven and earth and all things, my animal soul in the animal soul of

[1] William Littleboy, *The Appeal of Quakerism to the Non-Mystic,* 1916.

heaven and earth, my soul be merged into the soul of heaven and earth and all things as all different metals could be melted into one metal. It is thus that heaven and earth and all things are no more than my essence, my spirit, my animal soul and my soul. There is nothing that dies, there is nothing that is born."

Mysticism in Taoism takes the form of a divine reality which undergirds existence and is its motive power, like the Logos of Saint John. As Jesus taught that only the pure in heart would see God, so Taoism holds that only one who has purged his heart of desire and concentrated his mind can understand the mystery of Tao. The developed concept of Tao was of a nameless and transcendent source of all things and an immanent force which had entered and permeated the cosmos. By becoming emptied of self, a man can see the Tao in everything, and how throughout nature all things return to the source as the plants after blossoming return to the root and remain alive there.

In any religion, the deepest sense of the divine nature goes towards fullness, towards some All or Absolute bigger than the mind can grasp, and then experiments with methods by which—impossible yet paradoxically achievable—this All may be encompassed by the seeker. In India "Param-Atman" is the name given to this divine power which unites all existence. In Confucianism "t'ien" and "ti" (heaven and earth) are the great father and mother, through whom we are as much one substance with the universe as our bodies are the substance of our parents. So by symbolic parallel our natures partake of the nature of heaven. *Hsiao* (filial piety) is therefore not restricted to merely human relations, but to man's umbilical relationship to earth and heaven.

Mo-Tzŭ (Mo Ti or Micius, *c.* 468–382 B.C.), who followed Confucius, developed the idea of reciprocal love. "If the people would only practice reciprocal love," he wrote, "they would look upon the bodies of other people as their own, upon the homes of other people as their own homes, and upon the lands of other people as their own lands. Dissension and war between states would disappear, discord between homes would vanish, enmity between individuals would cease, and there would be full and universal harmony." A very commonsensical, practical way of putting the intuition of mystical oneness into effect!

THE UNIVERSAL RELIGION

In the Western world, mysticism goes back to Plato, who may have got it from Eastern origins and who found in the soul an "eye for divine Reality." Socrates often spoke of his inner sense or connection with the divine, and was led by his inner voice to walk the martyr's path. Even Aristotle assumes that man's power to reason is related to the divine reason which in the act of beholding, beholds itself.

The Stoics, who taught that there is a seed of God in the human soul, believed that the inner spirit by freeing itself from all particularities can identify itself with the universal reason.

Stoic ideas influenced the early Christians, who had already inherited from the teachings of Jesus a firm faith in personally experiencing the presence of God. Christianity is from the beginning a mystical religion, and only the encrustations of history have hidden this from us. The early church was clearly a mystic fellowship in which the members were bound together by the feeling of the divine presence in their assemblies.

Plotinus, gathering the great insights of classical philosophy, taught that God is the root of the soul. Out of God, who is a transcendent Unity, comes Mind which radiates from him as light from a luminous body, irradiating all minds, and Soul, which gathers and includes all individuals so that all souls are distinct and yet one. His famous phrase, "the flight of the alone to the Alone," expresses the mystic's sense of the divine that is within merged with the All.

Mysticism appeared again in the medieval church as a protest against excessive dialectic and disputation. So in the twelfth century Bernard of Clairvaux dealt with the means by which man might reach God through contemplation.

"As the little water-drop poured into a large measure of wine seems to lose its own nature entirely and to take on both the taste and the color of the wine . . . so must all human feeling towards the Holy One be self-dissolved in unspeakable wise, and wholly transfused into the will of God." (*De Diligendo Deo,* c. 10.)

Meister Eckhart, greatest of the German mystics, freed himself from scholasticism and developed his sense of oneness with the divine by free exercise of his own gifts of reason and imagination. Godhead, as he strikingly put it, is a "nameless Nothing" above all limitations or definitions. But the Godhead is revealed in God—the uttered Word, the divine expressed in personal form.

Nonsense In later mystics such as Saint Theresa and John of the Cross, mysticism has lost its bold speculations and become a repetition of sense images. With groups like the Friends of God, Seekers, and Quakers, mysticism, in line with the democratizing trend which went along with Protestantism, became again the heritage of every humble believer as it had been in the first Christian churches.

In Islam it was the Sufis who sought this oneness with the divine. They aimed at freeing the soul from all passions and evil instincts so that there would be no room in the heart for anything but God. The Sufi poet Attar, in a richly allegorical poem called "The Colloquy of the Birds," describes the mystic pilgrimage as a quest which begins with the stripping off of all earthly things and then progresses through love, knowledge, a sense of unity and amazement to annihilation of self.

In America, Emerson drew all these streams together—Christianity, Neoplatonism, German Transcendentalism, the sacred books of the East, the "inner light" of the Quakers—and with his firm, eloquent, seerlike voice reawakened a people whose orthodoxies were hardening and made them look inward again. Emerson saw that all was one—the Holy Ghost, the seed, the One of Plato or Plotinus, the Universal Mind of yogis and Sufis. On his walks around Concord he felt within himself the circulation of this divine current. Men must learn to trust this universal soul within themselves—this collective psyche, this Oversoul which gave a common heartbeat to all existence.

"I believe I shall some time cease to be an individual, that the eternal tendency of the soul is to become Universal, to animate the last extremities of organization," he wrote in his *Journal*.

And again: "How precisely parallel are the biographies of religious enthusiasts—Swedenborg, Guyon, Fox, Luther, and perhaps Boehmen. Each owes all to the discovery that God must be sought within, not without. That is the discovery of Jesus."

"Jesus was Jesus because he refused to listen to another, and listened at home." [2]

This universal element that Emerson both perceived in others and felt in himself is the ground of all religion as distinguished from religions. Hindu or Muslim or Christian set themselves apart by the names they give to God, by the doctrines they build around the teachings of their great founders. What religion unites, churches divide. The vision of every great religious teacher is a testimony to the unnameable oneness of the divine and its reachable presence within man. All rituals, doctrines, dogmas, institutions are but faulty human ways of trying—often perversely— to preserve this original insight. They are no more effective in keeping it alive than embalming preserves life in a body. They may preserve the features, but not the spirit.

In the mystic, that universal religion is preserved. Its qualities are the same, no matter whether the mystic is Hindu, Muslim or Christian, and no matter whether the time is 3,000 B.C., the years when Jesus walked the earth, or now. If only all men would

[2] *The Heart of Emerson's Journals.*

open themselves to the heritage that is within, practising through the discipline of meditation what all religious teachers recommend, they would be linked in a bond that could not be broken.

QUALITIES OF MYSTICISM

Several qualities distinguish mysticism wherever it is found.

1. *Consciousness*. Mysticism arises from a latent form of consciousness beyond intellect and emotion but drawing upon them and upon all the sensibilities and instruments of perception for a unified apprehension of all life, all being, experienced as a totality in which the perceiver himself is merged.

2. *Quiet*. As with meditation, the basis of mystical perception is silence. Jakob Boehme says that when will and intellect grow quiet, the soul can rise above temporal things; then the eternal hearing, seeing and speaking are revealed. The more the conscious mind can quiet itself and become passive, the more the divine mind can emerge. Quiet, to the mystic, is the truest, deepest activity.

3. *Love*. Anyone who has met a practising mystic has sensed the outflowing of light and love, childlike yet deeply mature, from the inner springs of his personality. It is by love that the mystic reaches God, and it is God's love that irradiates him. One of the surest signs of the essentially mystic nature of the religion Jesus taught is its centering on love.

Love is the bond between man and God. "Love may reach to God in this life, but not knowing," says the unknown author of *The Cloud of Unknowing*. "Go up towards that thick Cloud of Unknowing with a sharp dart of longing love."

This is always the message of the mystic. Give yourself to the divine, the infinite life, this mystery of which you are a part. Trust it. Let it well up in you.

Love, united to the will, can raise the self to a new level of perception which transcends the world of the senses. Then through love the seeker is joined to the object of his search.

"Thou has made us for Thyself, and our hearts can find no rest outside of Thee," says Saint Augustine. The mutual longing of man's spirit and God's are like iron filings sprinkled upon a paper resting on a magnet. Though the magnet cannot be seen, the particles are inevitably and unerringly drawn to the unseen and form a perfect pattern around it.

The language of the mystic often seems embarrassingly like that of the lover, and sometimes, as with the Sufis or with some of the Christian mystics, it is hard to tell the difference between religious and erotic writing. Indeed the committed mystic (often a celibate) seems like a young lover in his enthusiasm and devotion, his exaltation and his humility.

The German mystic Suso has an unforgettable passage in which he likens the mystic thirsting after the divine to a baby on its mother's lap.

"The baby, by the movements of its little head, and all its little body, tries to get closer and closer to its dear mother, and shows by its little laughing gestures the gladness of its heart." (*Leben,* cap. lv.)

4. *Union.* The thirst for union is the natural outcome of this motion of love, if indeed they can be separated. The one central teaching of the mystics is, as Eckhart put it, that man through the divine spark within his soul may rise into union with the Godhead in an Eternal Now.

"The Divine treasure lies hidden in thy own soul," wrote Walter Hilton in fourteenth-century England. "The piece of money—the groat—is lost in thy own house."

The Absolute of the mystic is not cold, distant, and unapproachable. When found, it is something both lovable and living.

Yet there are many testimonies to the difficulty of this discovery.

183

Meditation: The Inward Art

"There was never yet pure creature in this life, nor never yet shall be, so high ravished in contemplation and love of the God-head, that there is not evermore a high and wonderful cloud of unknowing betwixt him and his God," says the author of *The Cloud of Unknowing.*

"Then will He sometimes peradventure send out a beam of ghostly light, piercing this cloud of unknowing that is betwixt thee and Him; and shew thee some of His privity, the which man may not, nor cannot speak. Then shalt thou feel thine affection inflamed with the fire of His love, far more than I can tell thee."

The craving of the soul for its mate, often accompanied by a longing to achieve purity and perfection, breaks out in such a cry as this:

"I would fain be to the Eternal Goodness what his own hand is to a man." (*Theologia Germanica.*)

Often the radiant awareness of the "otherness" in nature, of Wordsworth's "something far more deeply interfused" is the first sign of mystical illumination. The radiance, flooding the whole personality as if with a new light, becomes apparent in the face and gestures of the enlightened. He is ready to cry with Angela of Foligno: "This whole world is full of God!"

Images of light inevitably come to the lips of those who have been enlightened. Paul, blinded with that light on the road to Damascus, often speaks in images of light: "God hath shined in our hearts." And John too: "That was the true Light, which lighteth every man that cometh into the world."

5. *Transcendence become Immanent.* The theorizing of theologians about God as transcendent and immanent, the cosmic God beyond knowing and the God within, does not concern the mystic. He will admit with Paul that God has shined into his heart, but he knows that God was already there—the divine seed, the inward light.

Rufus Jones says with all mystics, "God Himself is the ground of the soul, and in the deeps of their being all men partake of one central divine life." [3]

Is there anyone who has entirely escaped this feeling of inner joy and serenity? Perhaps it has come while watching a sunrise at sea, or upon stepping out into a bitter cold night and looking up at the stars, or as a fugue of Bach strides up to its noble climax. At such moments the larger presence is felt by any sensitive person, and by quiet meditation can be seized and held. Then we know that something is present in us beyond the ordinary self. In religious terms, we have felt the immanence of the divine: Emmanuel—God with us.

And there are times when we equally feel the presence of evil —the sudden fever of hate or anger, the temptation to belittle or ridicule the defenseless, to turn a shady profit, to betray a trust. But we know these things for evil and are ashamed of them, even if we do them. And we long and yearn for the good, knowing it for what it is and trying to beat the evil down in us as if it were a mad dog baring its fangs.

How are we so certain that one thing is evil and another good? How could we know the difference unless we are somehow firmly yoked to that goodness in which we recognize the divine?

"God is near us," says Meister Eckhart, "but we are far from Him; God is within, we are without; God is at home, we are in a far country." (*Pred*. lxix.)

When our motions are toward evil, the divine becomes distant —not by removing itself from us but because we wrap and muffle it with our indifference. Yet it is still there, within. This is the faith of the mystic, and it is a knowledge based upon experience. Not upon doctrine, dogma, creed, encyclical, or church. It is as real as what you see through a microscope, what you grasp with your hands, what you chew and swallow and digest. The literature of mysticism is full of bright and memorable images because mystics see, hear and feel with an intensity which

[3] *Studies in Mystical Religion*. London, 1909, p. xxxii.

vibrates to spiritual overtones. Spirit has cleared their vision, sharpened their senses, toned up their awareness. If the divine is ever-present, one must be keen of sense and quick of eye to take it all in.

Through the divine that is within and that has been experienced, one is led up to an intimation of the divine that is beyond knowing because if it were not beyond man's powers of understanding it would not be transcendent. Yet we are led to it by those inner leadings that are so real, we cannot doubt their authenticity. Like Moses, we may have to look on the promised land from a distance. But we know it is there; otherwise we would not be here.

THE MYSTIC EXPERIENCE

So much for the nature of the mystical experience. Now let us see what forms the experience usually takes.

Mystics have described the stages they pass through in various ways, yet the general lines do not vary much. The first stage is that of awakening—becoming tuned and ready; next, self-knowledge or self-examination; then illumination as the light breaks in and the sense of divine presence begins to flower; then surrender to the presence of the divine spirit, and finally union with it.

Many mystics speak of "the dark night of the soul" or "the cloud of unknowing" when they try to describe a feeling of stagnation which often comes after the period of illumination and before they feel united to the divine.

How do you go about the work of mystic contemplation?

Retire to a quiet place, relax and be at ease. Awaken yourself to what lies ahead. Warm yourself with anticipation.

If prayer is a natural form of expression for you, begin with that. Then meditation. The first stage is usually called recollection, or gathering of self, or self knowledge. This is a matter of being at ease with self in order to go beyond self. Then comes a period of quiet when the mind rests. It takes strength to hold the mind quiet and empty and to prevent it from playing with the scraps and bits of thoughts that keep rising. But from this quietness a thought will rise that is worth pursuing—perhaps a single word: peace. "Blessed are the peacemakers: for they shall be called the children of God." (Matthew 5:9.)

A vision of that hillside where Jesus spoke to the plain people who had come out to hear him may suddenly grow real. A sense of the presence of the divinely inspired person who spoke these words may follow—warm, exciting, close. At the moment when this presence is internalized, is felt as something within oneself, there will be a swift transition from meditation to contemplation.

Contemplation, as Evelyn Underhill says, is the mystic's medium. It is what harmony is to the musician, form and color to the artist, or rhythm to the poet. Whereas in meditation an idea is resolved and considered in the mind, in contemplation the object, whatever it may be—a prospect of mountains, a waterfall, a statue of Buddha or Jesus, a child playing, a deer browsing, an orchestra playing—is absorbed into the consciousness. The contemplator also lets himself be absorbed into the thing he is contemplating—not by reflective thought but by an effort to enter into it. In art, the experience is known as empathy.

The origin of the words "meditation" and "contemplation," remember, make the difference clear. "To meditate" is to measure, to consider all the aspects of a subject, while "contemplation" is to keep one's attention steadily upon a single thought. So the sense of the presence of Jesus may evoke an expansion of consciousness which transports the contemplator beyond himself into a state of oneness with the One, the divine, the cosmic. Through the sense of personal contact with the great teacher, the divine spirit, one enters into a sense of oneness with all that is holy. From the immanent to the transcendent is one leap, because they are one. What you feel to be divine within is one

187

with all that is divine. Down this radiant path the enlightened one walks with illumined face toward the source.

The types of mystic experience have been classified in different ways, but seem to resolve themselves into three:

1. Radiant apprehension of the Absolute, the One, the divine which comprehends both transcendent and immanent.

2. A new clarity of vision which makes all things shine and which gives a fresh significance to everything in the natural world. As George Fox put it in his Journal: "All things were new, and all the creation gave another smell unto me than before, beyond what words can utter."

3. A new internal energy which expresses itself in loving-kindness toward others, in an outgoingness which draws others within the divine circle, and in cheerfully giving of oneself.

I think any sincere and normally intelligent person who is willing to accept the disciplines of meditation can reach this level of mysticism. But there is the final stage of ecstasy, which differs from the Hindu *samadhi* only in that *samadhi* is sought as an end in itself while ecstasy implies the presence of a personally conceived deity.

Ecstasy occurs when the contemplator is cut off from the world of ordinary perceptions and responses and feels himself to be taken up into the One, the All, the Deity. Saint Catherine of Genoa described her experience (in the third person) as "a feeling of such utter peace and tranquillity that it seems to her that her heart, and her bodily being, and all both within and without is immersed in an ocean of utmost peace; from whence she shall never come forth for anything that can befall her in this life." [4]

The mystic who really succeeds in losing himself in contemplation, in merging his consciousness into the cosmic consciousness, also succeeds in finding himself. "The mystic has more and

[4] Quoted in Evelyn Underhill, *Mysticism*, New York, 1911, p. 528.

more the impression of being that which he knows and of knowing that which he is." [5]

One who identifies himself with all that he experiences seems to drink in power and courage and love from the encounter. He no longer feels helpless and alone, a cog in a vast machine. Rather, he partakes of everything, and all the powers and beauties of the natural world, from the smallest flower to the farthest star, are his powers and beauties. Transcendent and immanent are no longer theological terms creating an unbridgeable dualism in the divine itself. They are aspects of one power, one life, one experience. The life that flows through all things is his, for he is its.

Death and destruction are then seen as mercies, without which ugliness would be universal and the earth cumbered with decay. Even evil may appear as the goad without which good would die for lack of exercise. In all that flows and changes and dies, the mystic finds proof of something superior that contains all this—a womb in which life is cradled.

Rufus Jones, who was a practical as well as a practising mystic, believed that the mystic intuition should and could transform a person into a radiant and vital disciple of the goodness and the divinity his vision revealed to him. He called this affirmative mysticism, to distinguish it from that of the mystics who simply withdraw from the world and lose themselves in ecstasy and a secret experience of the divine. To him, mysticism provided the fuel for a man who was willing to cooperate in doing God's work.

"True godliness," wrote another Quaker, William Penn, "does not turn men out of the world, but enables them to live better in it and excites their endeavors to mend it."

"Those who see God," Rufus Jones said, "must gird for service. Those who would have a closer view of the divine must seek it in a life of love and sacrifice."

[5] *Etudes sur le Mysticisme.*

189

Meditation: The Inward Art

The insistence on combining an inner sense of the divine presence with active work in society has distinguished Friends throughout their history. They pioneered in prison reform, in care of the insane, in freeing slaves and in racial equality, in ministering to the homeless and dispossessed no matter what their religion, race or politics. The basis of this service is religious, not social and not humane. It arises from the assurance, gained experimentally, meditatively, directly, that man is one with God and that they have work to do together.

There is nothing incompatible about an inward mystical religion and an active outward life of service. Indeed they are all a part of one pattern, one weaving. For if life is one web, service to others is also self-service. "It is more blessed to give than to receive" might as well be "It is equally blessed to give and to receive," where both motions are necessary parts of one great action.

Eckhart nobly expressed the reciprocal nature of mystical insight and loving service when he said: "What a man takes in by contemplation he must pour out in love."

If the divine current runs through all life, a man may be charged with it wherever he chooses to plug in. The mystic sense of unity illuminates the world with a light in which we see that all problems are our own. Yet in giving us this vast burden to bear, it also gives us courage and power to shoulder it.

On this basis, the paradoxical words of Jesus about relieving men of their burdens, and then in the next moment offering them a yoke and a burden, and then assuring them that it is light—all this comes clear. It represents the vision of one who has seen the unity that is divine, and the service that is perfect freedom:

"Come unto me, all ye that . . . are heavy laden, and I will give you rest. Take my yoke upon you, and learn of me; for I am meek and lowly in heart: and ye shall find rest unto your souls. For my yoke is easy, and my burden is light." (Matthew 11:28–30.)

14

HOW OTHERS MEDITATE

I have read a great many meditations by seekers and religious writers of the past and present —enough to make an anthology of selections. But that is beyond the scope of this book. In Thomas Traherne's *Centuries of Meditations* I have found the most satisfying meditations of all, but that is of course a personal judgment. He avoids dogmatizing. He avoids creating the impression that he knows all the answers —a deadly error for meditation, which of its nature is a seeking for truth, knowing that we can unravel only fragments of it. He is able to convey a sense of joy and serenity as qualities which have grown within him, and which he shares with us. He is meek in the Biblical sense, and full of a light which he seems to reflect from a radiant inner source. Here are a few samples, each of which could be the beginning of a personal meditation.

"Love is so divine and perfect a thing, that it is worthy to be the very end and being of the Deity. It is His goodness, and it is His glory. We therefore so vastly delight in love, because all these excellencies and all other whatsoever lie within it." (II, 48)

"You never enjoy the world aright, till you see how a sand exhibiteth the wisdom and power of God. . . . Wine by its moisture quencheth my thirst, whether I consider it or no: but to see it flowing from His love who gave it unto man, quencheth the thirst even of the Holy Angels. To consider it, is to drink it spiritually. (I, 27)

"You never enjoy the world aright, till the Sea itself floweth in your veins, till you are clothed with the heavens, and crowned with the stars: and perceive yourself to be the sole heir of the whole world, and more than so because men are in it who are every one sole heirs as well as you. Till you can sing and rejoice and delight in God, as misers do in gold, and Kings in sceptres, you never enjoy the world." (I, 29) (How Traherne would have delighted to know as we know that the salt in our blood is indeed a survival of our prehuman sea life!)

"If you desire directions how to enjoy [the world], place yourself in it as if no one were created besides yourself, and consider all the services it doth unto you alone." (II, 2)

"To have blessings and to prize them is to be in Heaven; to have them and not to prize them is to be in Hell, I would say upon Earth: To prize them and not to have them, is to be in Hell." (I, 47)

"I evidently saw that the way to become rich and blessed was not by heaping accidental and devised riches to make ourselves great in the vulgar manner, but to approach more near, or to see more clearly with the eye of our understanding, the beauties and glories of the whole world: and to have communion with the Deity in the riches of God and Nature." (III, 67)

"How do we know, but the world is that body, which the Deity hath assumed to manifest His Beauty and by which He maketh Himself as visible, as it is possible he should?" (II, 20)

"God being, as we generally believe, infinite in goodness, it is most consonant and agreeable with His nature, that the best things should be most common. For nothing is more natural to

192

infinite goodness, than to make the best things most frequent; and only worthless things scarce. Then I began to enquire what things were most common: Air, Light, Heaven and Earth, Water, the Sun, Trees, Men and Women, Cities, Temples, &c. These I found common and obvious to all. Rubies, Pearls, Diamonds, Gold and Silver; these I found scarce, and to the most denied. Then began I to consider and compare the value of them which I measured by their serviceableness, and by the excellencies which would be found in them, should they be taken away. And in conclusion, I saw clearly, that there was a real valuableness in all the common things; in the scarce, a feigned." (III, 53)

FURTHER THOUGHTS FOR MEDITATION

And here are some more thoughts which may serve as useful starting points for meditation.

Out of this thorn experience I pluck the rose of truth.

From a Buddhist hymn: "As a mother, heedless of danger, stands between harm and her little one, her only child, let men, in their minds, embrace all living things. Let this embrace, unblemished by hate or ill will, include all the world, withholding naught." Quoted by Lester Mondale, *Values in World Religions,* Boston, 1958, p. 10.

"Avoid all evil, cherish all goodness, keep the mind pure. This is the teaching of Buddha."—Dwight Goddard, *A Buddhist Bible,* New York, 1952, p. 438.

"Since supreme omnipotence and perfect holiness are incompatible attributes, there is a note of rational absurdity in all religion, which more rational types of theologies attempt to eliminate. But they cannot succeed without sacrificing a measure of religious vitality."—Reinhold Niebuhr, *Moral Man and Immoral Society,* New York, 1932, p. 53.

"Patriotism transmutes individual unselfishness into national egoism. . . . The man in the street, with his lust for power and prestige thwarted by his own limitations and the necessities of social life, projects his ego upon his nation and indulges his anarchic lusts vicariously." *Ibid.,* pp. 91–93.

The first response to violence is anger and striking back. The second is rejection, shutting the door, cutting ourselves off. The first is brutish, the second childish. How do we learn the spiritual maturity of responding to violence with love?

Divine spirit, flame in the coal and spirit in the flesh, teach us to use the energy of our passions so that out of the black lump the flame will burn clear and strong, converting what is base and mean in us to what is noble and bright, for in the energy of our passions is a strength which can purify, and a power which can purge.

"Thou wouldst not seek Me if thou hadst not already found Me."—Pascal.

"Love is both a lever and a leveller."—Gurdial Mallik.

"We may be in the universe as dogs and cats are in our libraries, seeing the books and hearing the conversation, but having no inkling of the meaning of it all."—William James, *A Pluralistic Universe,* New York, 1909, p. 309.

"Be not conformed to this world: but be ye transformed by the renewing of your mind, that ye may prove what is that good, and acceptable, and perfect, will of God."—Romans 12:2. (Revised Standard Version: "Do not be conformed to this world but be transformed by the renewal of your mind, that you may prove what is the will of God, what is good and acceptable and perfect.")

"His will is our peace."—Dante.

"The man consists of his faith. He is verily what his faith is."
—Bhagavad-Gita.

"By the word God I mean an infinite substance, eternal, immutable, independent, omniscient, omnipotent, and that by which I myself and all other existent things . . . have been created and produced. . . . I would have no idea of an infinite substance, I who am a finite being, unless the idea had been placed in me by some substance which was in fact infinite."
—Descartes, *Meditations*.

"Of a truth I perceive that God is no respecter of persons: but in every nation he that feareth him, and worketh righteousness, is accepted with him."—Acts 10:34, 35.

If an enemy has harmed you, why harm yourself further by anger or plans for revenge? This is like grabbing a hot iron to hit someone—you hurt yourself first.

"The bad always rule over the good and always do violence to them. . . . Thus, whether political violence be abolished or not, the condition of the good men who are violated by the bad will not be changed thereby."—Tolstoi, *The Kingdom of God Is Within You,* Boston, 1951, p. 249.

O divine spirit, let us be as vessels filled with a due measure of thy gentleness and strength, loving kindness and forgiveness, understanding and love, joy and beauty, peace and quietness, so that we may pour them out in thy service until we become as living fountains of thy eternal purpose.

India at its best has a vision of universal truth through Brahman, the source of all. Japan's vision is of beauty and the esthetic sense as the governor of life. In the West, action for good is our chief vision. Can these three insights of truth, beauty and the good be combined? Can we, drawing upon Hindu, Buddhist and Christian cultures, as well as upon all religions, mold a brotherhood of devotion to this trinity which is beyond dogma, but established in experience? Through the direct appeal to experience practised by some branch of every religion, can we draw all men to share their insights on a universal plane?

"Will is a power through the which we choose good, after that it be determined with Reason."—*The Cloud of Unknowing,* London, 1912, p. 279.

"For not what thou art, nor what thou hast been, beholdeth God with his merciful eyes; but that thou wouldest be."—*Ibid.,* p. 314.

"There is a spirit which I feel that delights to do no evil nor to revenge any wrong, but delights to endure all things, in hope to enjoy its own in the end. Its hope is to outlive all wrath and contention, and to weary out all exaltation and cruelty, or whatever is of a nature contrary to itself. . . . Its crown is meekness, its life is everlasting love unfeigned; and takes its kingdom with entreaty and not with contention, and keeps it by lowliness of mind. In God alone it can rejoice, though none else regard it, or can own its life. It's conceived in sorrow, and brought forth without any to pity it, nor doth it murmur at grief and oppression. It never rejoiceth but through sufferings: for with the world's joy it is murdered. I found it alone, being forsaken. I have fellowship therein with them who lived in dense and desolate places in the earth, who through death obtained this resurrection and eternal holy life."—James Nayler at his death in 1660.

Life is a gift, not a right. Just as we quickly grow accustomed to our privileges and good fortune and think of them as our due, so we assume that we are entitled to perfect health and to life itself. But all life is a loan. We borrow it from the bank, and we have to pay it back, with interest. That is what makes it eternal. We need then to be grateful for whatever of life is granted us, since the alternative would be not to have had it at all. And we need to be ready and willing to relinquish it as one gives up his seat to a lady or vacates leased premises when the time is up.

"There is no way to peace; peace is the way."

Peace is not a political thing, but a spiritual. "Peace I leave with you, my peace I give unto you: not as the world giveth, give I unto you." (John 14:27.) Peace must begin from within, as a flower grows from seed to bud to bloom. The Buddhist idea is that peace comes through overcoming desire, and therefore comes chiefly to those who are either sainted or dead. In the Christian view, peace is an active, creative power to be sought and lived. But it cannot begin at the United Nations or in the world's capitals. It must begin in us. When we boil with anger over an affront or indignity, when we lie within a cold steel wall of frustration and hit out as if to even the score, here is where peace ends and strife begins.

How shall we nurture inner peace?

We begin with the sense that since all are united in one gift of life, there is no mine and thine. Loving others is a form of self-love, and it is love that casts out fear. Love generates peace;

peace is the condition of those who know how to love. "There is no way to peace; peace is the way."

A Japanese poem says:

> *O love, who gave thee thy superfluous name?*
> *Loving and dying, are they not the same?*

What a preposterous idea, on the surface! What can it mean?

It means, perhaps, that by love we overcome our selfish lower natures and learn to sacrifice to others, even unto death as Jesus did. We die unto selfishness and sin in order that we may live unto truth. In the death of the ego the greater, truer self is born.

Perhaps that is why the love-death is so potent a symbol in all literature and religion. The year king guards the sacred tree, but is murdered by the king of the wood who replaces him. The yule log is burned, not that it may perish but that the sun may be restrengthened and the new year bring on its new growth. The god is murdered in order to be reborn. "Unless it die, how shall it be quickened?"

But what of death? How can meditation help us here?

The Christian idea of immortality, a confused one, imagines a waking to a terrible Last Judgment Day when all shall be judged and rewarded, some with a blissful but rather disembodied life in heaven. The Muslim heaven is rather more tangible, with rewards such as the living might yearn for. The Hindu-Buddhist idea of karma—of life going on through one existence after another until perfection is attained—puts heaven very far away.

But are not all these heavens intended symbolically? How many Christians really believe that they will ascend to a place where they can live a life of eternal bliss? Or that they will go to hell?

Is not true immortality found in the trail we leave behind us

—in our children, our friends, the things we create, the work we do, the impact we have on our communities? This, indeed, is the true immortality of Jesus—that he lives in us. *Not acc to Jesus!*

In the total view, immortality is a social thing. We share it with all that has gone before, that has gone into the making of us, and all that goes after us which we have had a share in making. And if immortality is universal instead of particular, does this not elevate us to a life that is far grander than we deserve? Would we exchange it willingly for a pinched and narrow personal immortality?

We all fear death to some extent. In India, one of the aspects of god is Vishnu, the destroyer. How strange! Yet when we see the death of an old person who dies before falling victim to all the ills and indignities of the flesh, is it not clear that destruction is merciful, and that that which takes away life is as necessary and as divine as that which gives?

But what shall we think when a young mother dies? What goodness is there in that?

Our error is in trying to catch God in error. Disease and accident happen without regard to moral worth. The why of natural law is in its way as beautiful as a work of art. We need not blame God for viruses and cancer and car accidents. God is spirit, the embodiment of all that a good man knows how to conceive and more. He is not a whiskered grandfather watching over us and keeping harm away from us. We take our chances in this vast, splendid creation, and we have no right to ask that it be otherwise. God is the spirit who informs it, not the cop who swoops down to punish offenders.

Living is tough—that is one of its conditions. If we are willing to thank our Author for the gift of life, we cannot then beg him to change it from a sharp sword to a soft drink. The sword is both our spur and our protection. We have to be tough to face the blows, but thankful for the dear gift itself.

* * *

Meditation: The Inward Art

The following suggestions are adapted from *The Spiritual Exercises of Saint Ignatius*.

Call to mind the sins of your life, reviewing them year by year. (That seems to call for an unusually sharp memory!) Compare the attributes of God with the sins and shortcomings of the self—His power against your weakness, His goodness with your wickedness.

"There is a cry of wonder accompanied by surging emotion as I pass in review all creatures. How is it that they have permitted me to live, and have sustained me in life! . . . And the heavens, sun, moon, stars, and the elements; the fruits, birds, fishes, and other animals—why have they all been at my service!"

In imagination, visit the holy family after the birth of Jesus. "I will make myself a poor little unworthy slave, and as though present, look upon them, contemplate them, and serve them in their needs with all possible homage and reverence."

Consider humility, neither desiring riches nor poverty, honor or dishonor, a long life or a short one, except in order to serve God and the salvation of your soul more fully.

Think of a stranger whom you would like to see practise perfection, and what advice you would give him.

What way of life would you wish to have followed if you were at the moment of death? Or standing at the last day in the presence of your judge?

Return to God all that He has given you.

Consider how God dwells in all creatures—in the elements, in plants, in animals, in man.

With each breath, say one word of the Lord's prayer and concentrate upon its meaning.

15

SOME MEDITATIONS

UNITY

WHY is it that man cannot be satisfied with one, but must always try to improve upon it with two and three?

The Western mind has expended an incalculable amount of energy to build philosophical systems that assert duality as the bedrock of reality. Since Plato, at least, we have been busily cutting the world in two. Plato gave us ideas and not-being, Aristotle form and matter, Descartes thinking substances and extended substances, Kant the transcendental and empirical. Since Kant two dualisms, mind and matter, rational and empirical, have been tossed about from one philosopher to another, and the result is a very large heap of murdered words.

Christianity, not to be outdone by philosophers, has developed the doctrine of the Trinity, a thing Jesus never heard of, and has asserted that religious truth cannot exist outside this doctrine—which means that Jesus is beyond the pale, since he never taught it.

We try to distinguish mind and body—another two, or add spirit, which gives us three, and then try to puzzle out what this trinity of self may mean.

But can one really separate mind from body, or both from spirit? Medicine has at last found a word, psychosomatic, for that intimate interconnection of the mental and the physical which good doctors have recognized all along, and which systems like

Meditation: The Inward Art

Yoga take as their basis. Mind, body and spirit are one; the words are, after all, only abstractions which try to separate aspects of a unified organism. Often they fail even in this. Is a headache mental or physical? Is that thrill of identification and elevation that comes with music spiritual or physical? Is the feeling produced by a beautiful sunset physical, mental, or spiritual?

We know now—until the scientists tell us something else, at least—that what we call matter is really the motions of positrons, neutrons and other electrical charges within the structure of the atom. Energy and matter are not distinguishable as two: they are one. Metaphysics, theology and philosophy need to give up their dualisms as the natural sciences have done.

Our tendency to divide the world into sensate and insensate may be equally fallacious. Looked at from the totality, sensate beings and "inert" matter (all of it, as we now know, pulsing with energy, electrical forces and moving charges) are one. They are part of a deeper unity in which sensation is a part of matter. Matter seems less and less inert the more we learn about it. As the operations of the mind may be explained on a biochemical and biophysical basis, so it may be that matter will one day be seen to have a mind of its own as the distinctions between mind and matter break down. The randomness of the motions of interatomic charges already provides a hint.

So mind, body, and spirit are one complex unity. But the individual does not come into his full inheritance until his own mind-body-spirit is felt as one instance of universal Mind-Body-Spirit, just as each of these three aspects is part of an organic and inseparable whole individual. The whole individual is his own mind-body-spirit embraced within the Mind-Body-Spirit of the whole creation, from proton to star, from atom to galaxy.

Not dualism, not trinity, but complex unity. ✗

Body, mind and spirit. Object, use and user. Cell, genes, atomic structure. The creator, the work, and the audience. In

[handwritten: Cx unity =s △ , dum dum !]

202

each case the unity is what makes the meaning. One without the others is nothing.

Composer, music, hearer. Do we hear Bach with our minds, our bodies or our spirits? What in any case do we mean by spirit?

Spirit, let us say for a trial, is that which energizes matter. Well, but matter seems to be nothing much but energy now. Good. So much the better for our trend toward unity. In the world of physics matter is seen as an energy of forces within the atom. In the world of man spirit is the energy we perceive as truth, beauty or goodness—these three again united in a way we cannot fully understand (except perhaps as they are the manifestations of mind, body and soul), but which are so clearly fused in the life of Jesus, in a Euclidean proof, in a Bach Passion.

We assume a science that is beyond particular sciences which will approximate but never achieve truth. We assume an art beyond the particular painting or poem that will approach but never achieve perfect beauty. We assume a goodness beyond that of Jesus or Buddha that will never quite be fulfilled.

In Hindu thought, truth, beauty and goodness are held to be the three aspects of the soul.

The scientist probes the universe looking for truth, the artist for beauty, the moralist for goodness. All have faith in the truth, the beauty or the goodness they look for. Without this faith they could not work.

Inherent in the universe is a summation of all its meaning. If we could see it plain, we would perhaps then realize that truth, beauty and goodness are also only aspects of the total meaning. Yet our human limitations leave us always with a partial view. We are left with the paradox of unity in diversity, of error in good, of blemish in beauty, of truth that may be eternal but for us is progressive because it is being continuously revealed.

And we have to learn to be content with a situation in which our human limitations leave us with all these paradoxes, and with the knowledge that in all these paradoxes and beyond them is the unity we call God.

OF TIME, THE COMFORTABLE DIMENSION

The calendar of sidereal time is as the pocket watch of the Maker, and each of us is less than a single tick of eternity. Yet as we are bound into all, we are all. No one heartbeat is more important than another. Added together, they are life's clock. What if an individual life be but one pulsebeat of the universe? That beat is of equal importance with all the rest. Insofar as it partakes of the whole, it is the whole. The finger is of the body— it is the body. The individual is of the universe—he is the universe.

The nature of time is a mystery. The clock ticks off a mechanical sort of time, but only the mind can measure it significantly. A minute of danger may seem an hour; an hour of bliss may seem a minute.

Without time's flow, no experience is seizable. It is the comfortable dimension. Pain and sorrow would be insupportable without it; love and ecstasy gain their meaning from its motion.

There is a rhythm in nature that is time's metronome. Music is its art and symbol. The whole art of music is like a song to time, whose flow is essential to our being.

> *But at my back I always hear*
> *Time's wingèd chariot hurrying near,*
> *And yonder all before us lie*
> *Deserts of vast eternity.*
> —Andrew Marvell, *To his Coy Mistress.*

Time is as much a mystery as eternity; for what is eternity but time without the tick?

To the mystery of time's flow we have to add the miracle of

memory by which at the merest motion of the mind we reverse time.

When Stephen Foster died at thirty-eight in New York, his career drowned in drink, his family alienated, a scrap of newspaper was found by his bed. On it he had scribbled a few words which might have become another immortal song: "Dear friends and gentle hearts." In the squalor of his last moments, memory had returned him to the scenes and people of his promiseful youth—to his wife, Jane, their daughter Marion, the little cottage they had shared. Then for Foster the clock stopped and time without a ticking began. But the Foster of "Beautiful Dreamer" and "My Old Kentucky Home" goes on warming thousands of hearts.

The spiritual significance of time is that at any moment—here, now—we may have Gandhi, Plato, Lao Tse, Emerson with us. "Even so, come, Lord Jesus." And he comes. In us the past lives. What time separates, it also joins.

Meditation sets aside clocks and appointments, and carries time into the area of the spirit. Whenever the holy silence is established, we can summon up all that is great, letting it live again in us so that we are filled with it.

Yet even as we fill ourselves from the past, time goes on and we carry the past with us into the future. The present is therefore the place where past and future meet. And time is seen, not as three things but as one—as a continuum along which experience flows, occasionally reversing its motion.

In this sense we understand anew what Jesus meant when he said, "And, lo, I am with you alway, even unto the end of the world." (Matthew 28:20.)

OF LOVE, THE FIRST MOTION

In most primitive religions there is a god of love, and in his rituals love becomes god. But where there is a true love of God, men come to realize that God is love.

The dual law of love that Jesus taught—to love God, and thy neighbor as thyself—has three principals, God, neighbor and self. The key is really at the end: "Thou shalt love thy neighbor as *thyself.*" Self-love is the basis for all love—not in selfishness, but because in the self the all is most immediately and inescapably realized.

"The second is like unto it." Are the two laws of love like each other in the sense of being equally important, or in the sense of being really the same?

If the latter, another paradox is solved. God is love. We are to love God. So we are to love love. But this is meaningless until we see that the object fuses in the subject, the lover in the loved. The doer merges into his act, and the self merges into neighbor and into God.

WHERE IS GOD?

"I was glad when they said unto me, Let us go into the house of the Lord." (Psalms 122:1.)

"The Lord is in his holy temple: let all the earth keep silence before him." (Habakkuk 2:20.)

"And I will dwell in the house of the Lord for ever."

What is this house of the Lord? Where is it?

In the first two sentences it is clear that the house of worship is meant. But in the last, the Psalmist who has imagined himself as a sheep led into fresh pastures has clearly found that the earth is the Lord's and the fullness thereof, and that God is everywhere.

He dwells in it. But God is there because He is within. "That we may evermore dwell in him and he in us."

Silence is His dwelling place—beside the still waters, within the temple, within the self.

Nature is His dwelling place, the temple is His dwelling place. I am His dwelling place. I may be, only by willing it, a house of the Lord—a dwelling place for the most high, for goodness and truth and beauty. How simple! How wonderful!

Why do we go on being afraid of the name of the divine dweller, embarrassed to speak of God, fearful of being thought naive or hypocritical or opportunist? Can we not in one generous gesture throw overboard all the restraints and images of God we have brought with us from our youth, opening our minds to an idea, a surmise, a hope of a divine power that symbolizes the farthest scope of man's dream of the good? We must have a vision of God worthy to lead us; let us not be content with small gods—only with one beyond our grasp, yet near. Then we shall have a house to dwell in forever, and the silence within will be one with the silence of that space which is curved yet endless, and with a time that is timeless.

THE GRAND HYPOTHESIS

Let us suppose that we have to create a new world. Shall we make it all squares and circles, all alabaster and jewels—perfect, changeless, and therefore lifeless? Or shall we have life in it—leaves growing and rustling in the wind, animals creeping, flying, swimming, leaping, men loving, killing, sacrificing, dying?

Once we admit life into this world, we must admit suffering. There cannot be sentience, there cannot be ecstasy without pain. Pain is the warning bell which gives us the chance to save an injured foot, a burnt finger, or to preserve and mend a life that might otherwise be lost. There must be dying, because life involves birth and growth and decay; the only alternative is a granite world.

Assume the grand hypothesis—that there is some sort of current running through all life—in the stars and their courses, in gravity which keeps them and us orbiting, in the repetitive and integrated structure of every mite of matter with its ceaseless inner motion.

Suppose that cosmic rays, electric currents, X rays, radio waves, the current or wave within the atom, and that within the brain by which thought leaps to life are all in fact emanations of one great current.

Mind and matter are not then divorced; both operate on this current. Star and starfish are not separated; their orbits and their kinship are made manifest by telescope and microscope. Animate and inanimate are but variations on a theme. So life and death are necessary to each other. What we perceive in all mind, all matter, all space—the pulsing of what the scientist sees now as waves and then as particles—is the pulsing of one basically unified motion or energy or spirit.

It is not far or near, within or without: it is everywhere. His body is the universe. His mind is your mind and all minds. His strength is that of gravity in the wheeling planets or of Jesus on the cross. His nerves are the waves we call cosmic or those that wing back a message from outer space, or that announce our thoughts or sensations, or spin within each submicroscopic atom. This winging, this sensation, this pulsing of wave or current—is it not here that we sense the universal, supernal power?

On such a grand hypothesis we could stand free of provincial bondage to any one exclusive creed—united to all, joined to the infused power which energizes all that is, within and without, in the farthest heaven of the farthest star or in the haven of our hearts.

Then, having learned to see the spirit in matter, the heart in mind, the unity in variety, we would know not only that seeing is believing, but that believing is seeing. You have to believe in order to see anything. The more you believe, the more you see. The great visions, both in science and in religion, are based on faith.

A MEDITATION ON WORDS

Who spoke the first word? And how did the hearer understand it? How could a structure as intricate as language have grown in primitive minds?

This is a mystery, a miracle. No wonder that men have treated words as a form of magic. We have but to name the thing to have it appear to our minds. Words may emerge into acts, from the simplest "I will go shopping" to the terrible declaration of war. God's words are acts. "God said, Let there be light, and there was light." The nature of the divine is that word and act are one. The music of atomic motions, if we could hear it, is perhaps the universal language of pure energy manifest as pure sound.

Language—I mean a true language with all its subtleties and distinctions—is the miracle which marks man off from the beast. We know that we know, and this self-knowledge is a step towards the divine.

But words also have a divisive effect. Since it is the genius of language to distinguish and divide and thus to help the mind apprehend differences, its tendency is to make us habitual pluralists and thus to make us hostile to the idea of oneness.

Habit blinds us to the fact that words may falsify as they distinguish. We say "foreigner" or "Communist" or "immigrant" and immediately cut off a part of humanity from ourselves and cast them into darkness. We recall some childhood lesson that man is a combination of mind, body, and soul and forget that he responds as a total organism. We pretend that people are individuals and ignore the fact that they are part of a web whose strands are entangled in mud and stars.

Even nature we divide into inanimate, animate, and divine. Man, in the middle, is the bridge to unite the dumb beast with the divine word, the animal lust with the divine love, inanimate matter with divine immateriality. Mind is the bridge from matter to spirit, the perceiver of the link as well as the instrumental link itself.

Not all of theology can say what God is. But there is a sentiment within which knows the presence of the divine. It is a feeling, a knowledge beyond words. Only by growing through and beyond words can we come to a certain sense of the oneness in all. But words are our bridge to this knowledge too—a bridge like a rainbow, immaterial but apparent.

A MEDITATION ON SILENCE

In what language does the spirit speak?

An ancestor of mine in his old age learned Hebrew so that he might know the language "in which," as he wrote, "God, and angels, spake to the holy patriarchs, of old time; and what names were given to things, from the creation."

Yet the divine voice is not limited to Hebrew. There is also a language of silence, out of which most of all that voice may be heard.

The musician, the writer, the poet must first of all hear his work in the silence of his inner self. So the creative spirit speaks first in silence, and out of a silence that is filled like a vessel until it overflows into sound.

The moment of silence out of which the poem comes, or the idea, the prayer, the thanksgiving, the song—this moment with its quality of peace or light or radiance is as close as man ever comes to pure spirit.

"The Lord is in his holy temple; let all the earth keep silence before him."

Holiness and silence are closely united, and one often induces the other.

But this temple is the self. It is there that the radiance is felt, the voice heard. There only, for no matter what rituals and vestments and music may be concerted to induce a spirit of religion, the spirit must be present within or the acts of worship are as sounding brass and tinkling cymbals. Often, indeed, the perfunctory services we call religious drive away more worshipers than they collect and squash more true religion than they inspire.

"Make a joyful noise unto the Lord, all ye lands. Serve the Lord with gladness: come before his presence with singing." (Psalms 100:1, 2.)

The song follows the silence. The song is conceived in silence. The first language of the spirit is silence. If we listen with sensitiveness and anticipation, we shall hear the song in the silence. For in every silence there is a song. In the stillness and out of the stillness the spirit speaks.

THE CERTAIN TRINITY

The universal trinity is that of nature, man and the divine.

Most people come closest to a sense of oneness with the world when they are outdoors. Gardening, hiking, boating, or fishing restores that lost contact with earth and nature which men need in order to be whole.

Out of this contact with nature religion sprang, for it was his urge to make the crops grow that gave rise to man's invention of rituals that would imitate the creativeness of nature and thus encourage the repetition of the yearly miracle of spring.

When you think of the great moments of man's religious history, they all seem close to nature. The golden bough is the magical symbol of creativity that must be guarded even at the risk of life. Even sophisticated Greece puts its gods on Mount Olympus and keeps them in a pastoral setting. India's Krishna involves himself with milkmaids and cattle. Moses deals with sea and serpents and desert on his route to the mountain where

Meditation: The Inward Art

God speaks. God places His laws upon pieces of stone, or speaks from a bush. Jesus, as if to emphasize his oneness with nature, is born in a stable and cradled in a manger. His teachings get their clarity and humanity from their humble everyday quality as they speak of shepherds and sheep, loaves and fishes, vineyards and gardens.

The Twenty-third Psalm, which is so many things, perfectly expresses this trinity of nature, man and God. God Himself is the shepherd, and life is seen as a passage through still waters, green pastures, and the valley of death. In the presence of a bountiful nature and a loving God, man's cup runneth over; he has the experience of bliss, of ecstasy, the sense of oneness with the material, natural world and also with the divine. This is what it means to dwell in the house of the Lord.

This trinity is the basis of our political liberties, according to no less an authority than our Declaration of Independence. The "separate and equal" station to which any people are entitled comes to them through "the Laws of Nature and of Nature's God."

So it is through nature that we find pathways to the divine.

"I was glad when they said unto me, Let us go into the house of the Lord." (Psalms 122:1.) But the house of the Lord is not only church or synagogue or temple. It is also the mountaintop, the forest, the lake, the ocean. Not in the fire or in the whirlwind, but in a still small voice onward came the Lord. As Wordsworth puts it,

> *And I have felt*
> *A presence that disturbs me with the joy*
> *Of elevated thoughts; a sense sublime*
> *Of something far more deeply interfused,*
> *Whose dwelling is the light of setting suns,*
> *And the round ocean and the living air,*
> *And the blue sky, and in the mind of man;*
> *A motion and a spirit, that impels*

> *All thinking things, all objects of all thought,*
> *And rolls through all things.*
> > —*Lines Composed a Few Miles Above*
> > *Tintern Abbey.*

The house, the temple is within us. It must be there before we can find it elsewhere. The holiness we find in church or forest is something we already know, or we could not recognize it. "The kingdom of God is within you." This is what meditation works to make clear, but it cannot work from nothing. If it is not there, it is nowhere. If it is there, it will be everywhere, "where'er you walk."

Whatever is known of the divine, of religion, must be known within, "experimentally."

"This I knew experimentally," said George Fox of his religious enlightenment. It is the only way we can know religion or anything else, and meditation is the road to that knowledge.

Plotinus, finding an analogy in the Greek theater with its chorus placed around a choragus, or choral leader, says that when the singers turn away from the leader they sing out of tune, but when they turn to him they sing in perfect harmony. "So it is with us; we are always gathered around the divine center of our being." (*Ennead,* VI, 9, 8.) Looking inward—self-realization—is a discipline of discovery of the divine. Jesus had to spend forty days in the wilderness. Buddha had to seek for six years. The ancient forest sages of India devoted their lives to it. How many of us are willing to spend fifteen or twenty minutes a day?

Yet the fruits of such a search are testified over and again by those who have tried it. George Fox traveled up and down England looking for a religious teacher who could convince him.

"I saw that there was none among them all that could speak to my condition," he wrote in his Journal. "And when all my hopes in them and in all men were gone, so that I had nothing outwardly to help me, nor could I tell what to do; then, Oh! then I heard a voice which said, 'There is one, even Christ Jesus, that can speak to thy condition;' and when I heard it, my heart did leap for joy . . . and this I knew experimentally."

If religion is not continuously refreshed by this turning within, it withers. The cheerfulness, the overflowing of joy and love we see in truly religious people and in no one else—where does it come from? What do they possess that is beyond our reach? Where do they find it?

They find it within, "experimentally." There is no other way.

Jeremy Taylor, speaking of "The Practice of the Presence of God," says:

"God is wholly in every place; included in no place; not bound with cords except those of love; not divided into parts, not changeable into several shapes; filling heaven and earth with His present power and His never absent nature; and we can no more be removed from the presence of God than from our own being." (*Holy Living,* London, 1930, p. 22.)

"In the face of the sun you may see God's beauty; in the fire you may feel His heat warming; in the water His gentleness to refresh you: He it is that comforts your spirit when you have taken cordials, it is the dew of Heaven that makes your field give you bread." (Page 26.)

Says George Santayana in *Reason in Religion:* "God has no need for natural or logical witnesses, but speaks himself within the heart, being indeed that ineffable attraction which dwells in whatever is good and beautiful."

In nature and in human nature, in what surrounds us and what is within we find the materials and the equipment for meditation. And in meditation we transcend them. We become more than ourselves. Sunsets become more than mere daubs of color in the sky. The flower the maple puts out ahead of its leaf becomes more than a fragile, spindly mess of chlorophyl. Life is infused with wonder and with joy.

> *To me the meanest flower that blows can give*
> *Thoughts that do often lie too deep for tears.*
>   *—Ode: Intimations of Immortality.*

A MEDITATION ON THE NATURE OF GOD

In India gods in human form ride upon the backs of animals, clear evidence of the way anthropomorphic gods replaced the animistic ones. In more than one religion the protective, fertile mother-god has given way to the just and punishing father-god who in turn has made way for the god within. Religions change and grow; men mature; but the quest goes on. Perhaps the quest for God is the surest evidence of His being.

Men have identified the good with God. If God were only man's dream of the good, he would still be indispensable. Yet we are always worrying about proofs of his existence. We cannot see a thought, a feeling, a thrill to beauty, yet we do not doubt their authenticity. For we know them internally, experimentally. We cannot see air, yet we can fill our lungs with it and know it is there. In the same way, if at all, we come to know God. We can breathe Him and feel His presence—the allness in all, the nothingness in nothing, the animating force.

While we worry about proving His existence, He sustains ours. We doubt, and He is in the doubt. We think, and He partakes in the miracle of thought.

Western civilizations have exalted man and logic. The West tends to see all things as proceeding out of the mind of man, or at least to regard as significant only those things that are subject to logical proof. It says in effect, "I will believe in God so far as I can prove his existence." In India the basic assumption is quite different. "God exists. From this we prove existence; all things proceed out of God." The West is scientific, the East (the Old East, anyway) religious.

We keep worrying about the eroding effect that science has upon religion. The indifference of many to religion comes from the fact that we have made science our religion. "It's a scientific fact . . ." is our most compelling argument, even though we keep discovering that scientific facts have a way of quickly growing outmoded. In order to be "modern" we must be scientific, and to be scientific we must abandon religion. This is the vulgar error our civilization has fostered.

Yet we fail to use the scientific, the experimental method in our religion. We easily reject outmoded scientific theories for new without rejecting science, but insist on identifying religion with its outmoded theories and then reject all religion. How unscientific!

Once matter seemed "real" enough. Now we know it to be mostly a form of energy. Matter has evaporated from the material and we are quite willing to accept the scientist's assurance that it is imperceptible particles of energy in rapid motion. Yet we balk at the concept of immaterial divine force, whose presence is fully as well attested as that of protons and neutrons, since it has been realized "experimentally" by many religious people.

As science familiarizes us with the idea that matter itself is mostly energy, we ought to be capable of understanding that the energy we call spirit-energy is its highest form.

There is a truth that lies beyond scientific theories and religious doctrines which are always being disproved and outmoded. Religion should welcome every discovery of science, which in rolling back the boundaries of the known world makes the miracle of creation that much more wonderful, that much more divine. Personal religion, like science, should always be rolling back the boundaries—making new discoveries, discarding inadequate concepts, enlarging its vision.

Every religion has fallen short of its purest concepts by making God something less than spirit. The taint of anthropomorphism still clings to our own thinking, embarrasses us, and often persuades us to throw out religion instead of throwing out such a childlike concept. As if we were to abandon science because Einstein had exposed the errors of Newton.

True religion is not to be caught in a creed. It is that which an individual can accept on the basis of his own experience. "This I knew experimentally."

"God is a Spirit: and they that worship him must worship him in spirit and in truth." (John 4:24.) We may think of spirit as a form of energy which is perfectly realized through concept and act—the energy that informs energy, the life that gives life. Or, if we are not afraid of the word, God.

A MEDITATION ON THE NATURE OF DIVINITY

I do not know what God is. When I was a small boy, and my father took me every Sunday on a longish journey to the church he was serving as lay reader, and when he knelt in the chancel to pray, then I knew what God was. He was a kind of super-father whom even my father had to call father.

I do not know what God is. But when I grew somewhat older, and when at Christmastime the tree was brought into the house, smelling sweet and fresh from the woods, and when we covered it with tinsel and colored balls, and all the members of both families filled the living room for the giving of gifts, and then we walked through the snow to a midnight service and heard the Christmas story read from the altar, then too I knew what God was—the promise of birth and innocence and joy.

I do not know who God is. But when I became an acolyte and knelt upon the very altar steps while the minister read the Communion Service, it seemed to me that God himself was floating like a presence in the high ceiling over our heads, and I dared not look up.

And when I came to that age where everything must be embraced to be understood, and I wandered in woods or looked up at the purple hills of autumn, then too I knew what God was: it was the oneness of all created things, and the unifying presence of the life that was in them.

And when for the first time I felt that strange drawing towards one of the other sex, and was so drawn that I became silly and was so pleased with myself that I had to keep telling myself it was love, then too I knew the meaning of God.

And when our child came and I held him newborn in my arms and looked into the wide-staring, unseeing eyes still groping for life, then with this new life throbbing in my arms I came as close as ever to knowing what God the creator is.

And when my father's life was done and I stood by the quiet coffin and remembered the past, and those I had never known came and told me of this or that good thing he had quietly done for them, then again I felt a closeness to the God he believed in.

Endangered in the air, or tossing in a typhoon, or lying in the warm sun, or climbing a big tree, or breasting a storm, or listening to Bach and Mendelssohn and Handel, or reading Robert Frost or John Donne or Emily Dickinson, then too I have felt the closeness of the divine breath upon my neck.

I still do not know who God is. But I think that perhaps he, and she—for why should we always leave out one half of nature when we speak of the divine?—I think that all these things if they are added together may be as the hem of the garment of the spirit and the presence that is divine.

A MEDITATION ON THE MIRACLE OF THE COMMONPLACE

We live in a world of miracle. If the sun once failed to rise or the leaves failed to return one spring, we would think it a miracle when next they came. But because they are regular, we take them for granted. Yet the most miraculous things are the most regular—the beating of the heart, the certainty of night, the migration of birds. In these regularities we perceive laws—"the Laws of Nature and of Nature's God," as our Declaration of Independence puts it. What is more miraculous than that our world should operate by law? We are begotten and born and sustained by the most amazing complex of events, all subject to law. Law is miracle, and the greatest miracles are those we regard as commonplace. The great commonplace which we take so readily for granted is the miracle of the presence of the divine, exposed for us in the regularity of the Laws of Nature and of Nature's God. We do not need to wait for miracles, for we are surrounded with them, as every child knows.

Maturity too often brings a hardening of the perceptions which blinds us to miracle. Why did Jesus say that children were of the kingdom of heaven? Perhaps because he saw them perceiving the miracles to which their elders had grown insensitive. It is the sense of wonder at life, the sense of the miraculous, the sense of the divine in all the phenomena and manifestations of life that places the child close to heaven. To lose this sense of wonder is to lose contact with divinity. To preserve it is to keep the doorway open so that the light may flood in, together with the breeze, the song and the scent of a world that is all miracle.

IS THERE A GOD? A MEDITATION

Most of us are too busy or too scared to ask ourselves what we really think about the existence of God. And many who vaguely suspect there is no God are afraid to say so. A good many of these people probably go to church on Sunday.

Every man owes it to himself to know what he thinks. But he can only find this out by asking himself—which means meditation. And few are willing to take time for meditation. So not many people really know what they think.

The best place to begin is in the assumption that there is no God. Assume that the world is all matter and no spirit—that matter somehow made itself and that man is one of the end products of the slow evolution of matter from burning gases to the creation of planets, oceans, one-celled life, plants, animals.

The trouble is that all existence is so obviously structured, planned, and operated by laws that men are still discovering. And the more they discover, the more of a miracle the whole creation appears.

219

Meditation: The Inward Art

Creation? I cannot use that word if I am an atheist. Well, then, force or energy. What force or energy? I am assuming a purely mechanical world. Force and energy are mechanical terms, but they imply a source. We know from the laws of thermodynamics that energy cannot be destroyed. But where did it all come from? What name shall we give to the inconceivably vast force that brought the universe into being? How do we account for this orderliness and mind in the material world, to say nothing of the mind in animals and man?

How do we account for the fact that man knows good from evil, even when he does evil? And what shall we do with the historical evidence of God in history—of His role in finding the Jews a promised land, in the growth of civilization in India or China, in the remarkable spread of Islam—yes, even in the horrid religious wars and frightful inquisitorial tortures in His name? Even if we still insist that there is no God, we have to admit that men have acted as if He exists and have shaped their lives around Him—have bet their lives that He *is*.

Who are the great shapers of the Human tradition? Jesus, Socrates, Saint Augustine, Saint Paul, Asoka, Newton, Shakespeare, Dante, Milton, Lao-tse, Mohammed. Few atheists have had any important impact on human history. The Communists, of course. But even they have had to borrow all the paraphernalia of religion and devise ways to catch men's minds in a net of materialistic faith. Communism is hardly a religion, but it is a faith. Even its oversimplification of fact, its emotional appeal, and its quick denunciation of those outside the fold are easily recognizable.

Materialism does well enough up to a point. But it seems to be rather unsatisfactory in dealing with beginnings or ends. Or with things like the *St. Matthew Passion* of Bach, or *Tristan und Isolde,* or the impact of sunsets or moonlight on the human apparatus, or Jesus on the cross, or the Taj Mahal, or the Parthenon, or *King Lear* or a thousand other things one might name.

Matter does have a plan, a design behind it and all through it—so intricate, so beautiful, so unified that only great minds can grasp at it and smaller ones can only wonder. Existence is a miracle—all the more so if you insist it was all by chance. Life does contain within itself an evolutionary drive toward improvement and betterment which implies a purpose and a goal. Man does at times, either in the manner of Einstein or Mendelssohn or Robert Frost, have intimations of the grand design, the deeper meaning. Now and then a man or a woman comes along in whom something shines. Mankind, in all its cruelties, yearns toward good.

What shall we call this transcendence of the material, this quality of the material to soar beyond itself? If God seems too personal, too paternal, too bound up in childhood beliefs no longer tenable, call it the divine, the radiant, the spirit. But don't throw it away.

Since God is the symbol of man's dream of the good, what would it matter if the idea originated with man?

16

POSTSCRIPT

IT seems only fair to the reader that I should in a postscript tell where I stand—not to entice him to the same ground but that he may protect himself against the lines of force I have set up and, if he wishes, push the other way.

I am a Quaker by convincement. Having been born and raised in another church which gave me many rich experiences, a love of ritual, and a familiarity with the Bible, I therefore feel at home in other Christian groups. Having lived in Japan and India, I feel a deep respect and affiliation for Buddhist, Hindu, Sikh and Muslim insights.

A few years ago an Indian wrote to the *Friends Journal,* a Quaker publication, to point out that one of its issues had asserted a Quaker kinship with four non-Christian religions. A Hindu writing on Quakerism had found that the two faiths were essentially the same. Someone who had lived with the Hopis found that they shared with Quakers a feeling for peace and mutuality. A couple who had studied Islam reported that the similarities with Quakerism were more important than the differences. Someone who had talked with Buddhist Prime Minister U Nu of Burma found "a man whose underlying motivation is closely akin to that of a true Friend."

Quakerism, the Indian writer continued, is not a church or a creed; it is, like the core of any religion, a way of life. As the Bhagavad-Gita had recognized three ways to realize God—by adoration, knowledge, and action—so Quakers in their Meetings for Worship, their schools and their service committees have found a balanced, threefold way of life.

That pretty well expresses my reasons for being a Friend. There are others, of course. I might never have become a Friend if my wife had not been born one. When I felt unable to accept any longer the creed and ritual of my own church, I stayed away from all. It was only when I realized that within the Religious Society of Friends I would be free to find my own way to a sense of the divine and yet be given staunch support along the way—a support I could literally feel in the silent Meeting—that I knew where I belonged.

I felt a new air of freedom. I could think and meditate and conclude as I liked. All about me were others, occupied with their own searching. Occasionally someone spoke, and often, as Friends say, he "spoke to my condition." I discovered a corporate worship which was not by the book but in which each contributed his own particular insight, the product of his unique personality.

To me, the silent Meeting is the simplest, deepest and most rewarding form of worship ever devised. Every person present is taking an active part in it, whether he speaks or remains silent. Each presence is important. Whatever is said enters deeply into all because it comes out of an inner seeking. It comes fresh and true and felt. (Of course there are statements which seem uninspired, but these too have their uses. And they may not strike others as flat.) The habit of reflection takes hold. Daily meditation is easier because of the Meeting for Worship. It is more meaningful because one can meditate as if in Meeting, as if speaking to the condition of someone else as well as to and for oneself.

Quakers seek to serve that of God in every man. A small group—hardly 120,000 altogether in the United States, and divided into many Yearly Meetings including some which employ a pastor and conduct church services—they have nevertheless done a good deal in the way of meeting human needs. Not to relieve suffering for its own sake but to minister to that of God in man, so that others may also have a chance to realize the divinity within.

They believe that peace on earth is God's will and that it can be achieved. Their work for peace takes many forms—assistance to the war-torn, the refugee of whatever race or creed; international seminars to help students think about ways to peace; interracial work camps where young men and women from many countries can work with the disadvantaged to build better lives; conferences for young diplomats where world issues can be discussed frankly and without publicity; centers where international students, diplomats and world government people as well as men and women of all religions can have meaningful exchanges of ideas. Having spent nearly two years in charge of such a center in India, my wife and I have had a taste of what a world would be like in which such exchanges were the rule instead of the exception.

So I am a Quaker because I feel close to all the world's religions, and able to meet them on a common ground, unfettered by any restrictive creed or assertion of my own religious superiority. I am a Quaker because I feel both liberated and stimulated to seek that of God in every man and to serve it. And I am a Quaker because in meditation I come to grips both with that which I am and might be, and learn to grow toward the knowledge and love of the divine within and beyond, and in the bond of fellowship with all men everywhere.